DRAMA CLASSICS

The Drama Classics series aims to offer the world's greatest plays in affordable paperback editions for students, actors and theatregoers. The hallmarks of the series are accessible introductions, uncluttered and uncut texts and an overall theatrical perspective.

Given that readers may be encountering a particular play for the first time, the introduction seeks to fill in the theatrical/historical background and to outline the chief themes rather than concentrate on interpretational and textual analysis. Similarly the play-texts themselves are free of footnotes and other interpolations: instead there is an end-glossary of 'difficult' words and phrases.

The texts of the English-language plays in the series have been prepared taking full account of all existing scholarship. The foreign language plays have been newly translated into a modern English that is both actable and accurate: many of the translators regularly have their work staged professionally.

Under the editorship of Kenneth McLeish, the Drama Classics series is building into a first-class library of dramatic literature representing the best of world theatre.

Series editor: Kenneth McLeish

Associate editors:

Professor Trevor R. Griffiths, *School of Literary and Media Studies, University of North London*

Simon Trussler, *Reader in Drama, Goldsmiths' College, University of London*

DRAMA CLASSICS *the first hundred*

The Alchemist
All for Love
Amphitryon
Andromache
Antigone
Arden of Faversham
Bacchae
The Bad-tempered Man
The Beaux Stratagem
The Beggar's Opera
Birds
Blood Wedding
Brand
The Broken Jug
The Changeling
The Cherry Orchard
Children of the Sun
El Cid
The Country Wife
Cyrano de Bergerac
The Dance of Death
The Devil is an Ass
Doctor Faustus
A Doll's House
The Duchess of Malfi
Edward II
Electra (Euripides)
Electra (Sophocles)
An Enemy of the
    People
Enrico IV
The Eunuch
Every Man in his
    Humour
Everyman
The Father
Faust
A Flea in her Ear
Frogs

Fuenteovejuna
The Game of Love and
    Chance
Ghosts
The Government
    Inspector
Hedda Gabler
The Hypochondriac
The Importance of
    Being Earnest
An Italian Straw Hat
The Jew of Malta
King Oedipus
Life is a Dream
The Lower Depths
The Lucky Chance
Lulu
Lysistrata
The Magistrate
The Malcontent
The Man of Mode
The Marriage of
    Figaro
Mary Stuart
The Master Builder
Medea
Menaechmi
The Misanthrope
The Miser
Miss Julie
Molière
A Month in the
    Country
A New Way to Pay
    Old Debts
Oedipus at Kolonos
The Oresteia
Phaedra
Philoctetes

The Playboy of the
    Western World
The Revenger's
    Tragedy
The Rivals
The Robbers
La Ronde
The Rover
The School for Scandal
The Seagull
The Servant of Two
    Masters
She Stoops to Conquer
The Shoemaker's
    Holiday
Six Characters in Search
    of an Author
Spring's Awakening
Strife
Tartuffe
Thérèse Raquin
Three Sisters
'Tis Pity she's a Whore
Too Clever by Half
Ubu
Uncle Vanya
Vassa Zheleznova
Volpone
The Way of the World
The White Devil
The Wild Duck
Women Beware
    Women
Women of Troy
Woyzeck
Yerma

*The publishers welcome
suggestions for further titles*

DRAMA CLASSICS

THE DEVIL
IS AN ASS

by
Ben Jonson

introduced by Simon Trussler

NICK HERN BOOKS
London

in association with the

ROYAL SHAKESPEARE COMPANY
Stratford

A Drama Classic

This edition of *The Devil is an Ass* first published in Great Britain
as a paperback original in 1995 by Nick Hern Books Limited,
14 Larden Road, London W3 7ST

Copyright in the introduction © 1995 Nick Hern Books Limited

Text reproduced from the 'Revels Plays' edition of
The Devil is an Ass, Peter Happé (ed.), Manchester
University Press, 1994. By permission.

Typeset by Country Setting, Woodchurch, Kent TN26 3TB
Printed by BPC, Hazell Books Limited, Aylesbury HP20 1LB

A CIP catalogue record for this book is available from the
British Library

ISBN 1 85459 268 8

Introduction

Ben Jonson (1572-1637)

Ben Jonson was born just eight years after his near-contemporaries
Shakespeare and Marlowe – and a month or so after the death of his
father. His mother remarried – a master-bricklayer – in young Ben's
early childhood, and, although 'brought up poorly', the boy received
a good education at Westminster School under William Camden, his
lifelong friend. But instead of going on to university (a lack he always
regretted) he was reluctantly apprenticed to his stepfather's trade.

He escaped by volunteering to fight for the Dutch against the
Spanish in the Netherlands, then, in 1597, returned to London
to become an actor and playwright under the manager Philip
Henslowe. Not very happily married, and several times imprisoned –
once for killing a fellow-actor in a duel, twice for overstepping the
bounds of permissible satire in his plays – he none the less estab-
lished himself at court following the accession of James I in 1603.
Throughout his long subsequent career he alternated between
writing masques and entertainments for the King and his circle and
roistering comedies of London life for the public playhouses of his
native city.

Unlike Shakespeare, Jonson became a freelance, unattached to
a theatre company, and his livelihood remained precarious until,
in 1616, he was granted an annual pension and became (in effect)
the first Poet Laureate. *The Devil is an Ass*, written in the same year,
was thus his last play for the public stage until 1626, when he found
himself less favoured at court following the succession of Charles I.
His later comedies were not much enjoyed, and in 1628 a paralytic
stroke confined him to his chambers: but he kept on writing – and
entertaining his 'tribe' of disciples – to the end. After some years of
increasing destitution, he died in 1637 and was buried, standing up,
in Westminster Abbey.

What Happens in the Play

At the urging of a junior demon, Pug, Satan reluctantly agrees to let him spend one day in London, but denies him even the aid of the senile vice, Iniquity. Taking over the body of a recently hanged thief, Pug becomes servant to a squire from Norfolk, Fitzdottrel, who doesn't believe that Pug is a devil but is happy that he asks no wages. Bribed with the offer of an expensive cloak from Wittipol, Fitzdottrel allows this rival to woo his beautiful but mistreated wife Frances for just fifteen minutes, in his own jealous presence. Frances, though impressed by Wittipol's sympathetic eloquence, remains silent.

Merecraft, with his assistants Engine and Trains, successfully interests the gullible Fitzdottrel in the profits to be made from a project for reclaiming the drowned land of the Fens – of which he also promises to have Fitzdottrel made duke. Pug tries ineptly to seduce Frances, who packs him off with a coded message of encouragement for Wittipol. The spurned devil reveals the assignation to his master, who cuts short Wittipol's largely verbal advances to his would-be mistress. Merecraft suggests that Frances needs coaching in the behaviour proper to a potential duchess and persuades Fitzdottrel into buying an expensive ring to secure the services of a Spanish lady, reputedly skilled in teaching fashionable behaviour.

We now meet Gilthead, the goldsmith who is to supply the ring – and who plans to elevate his son, the more cautious Plutarchus, to the gentry. Merecraft and his aggressive cousin Everill persuade Wittipol, for his own amusement, to play the role of the 'Spanish lady'. This he does, greatly impressing both Lady Eitherside, the magistrate's wife, and her friend Tailbush, a female counterpart to the 'projector' Merecraft. Wittipol's friend Manly recognises the imposture: but he says nothing and, disabused of his amorous interest in Tailbush, departs in disgust, while Wittipol waffles glibly away about the mysteries of cosmetics.

Fitzdottrel is entranced by the 'Spanish lady', and not only puts his wife under 'her' tutelage but gives her Pug, to be trained as a lady's usher. Advised to settle his affairs against a fatal outcome of his intended duel with Wittipol, the besotted Fitzdottrel wants to make over his entire estate to the 'Spanish lady', but 'she' persuades him to name Manly as trustee instead. Once the documents are signed Wittipol, who has told Frances that he now wants only to be her virtuous friend, reveals himself to the enraged Fitzdottrel, who plots with Merecraft how to recoup his losses.

Gilthead and Plutarchus arrive with sergeants to arrest Fitzdottrel and Merecraft for the money they are owed, but Gilthead is diverted by the promise of a monopoly in the marketing of forks. The officers leave instead with Pug, who has stolen the fine clothes of Lady Tailbush's usher, Ambler, while he was dallying with a whore. The humiliated devil is thrown into a Newgate cell – from which he is rescued by an infuriated Satan and carried back to Hell by Iniquity amidst much venting of fire and brimstone. Fitzdottrel, who has meanwhile been feigning demonic possession to persuade Justice Eitherside that his wife bewitched him into making over his estate, abandons the pretence when the reports from Newgate convince him that he has indeed been harbouring a devil. Manly assures Fitzdottrel that the trusteeship will do him no harm, so long as the interests of his wife are protected, and urges the other rogues to repent: but nobody is to be exposed or punished.

The Theatres of Ben Jonson

Already, by the early years of the seventeenth century, Jonson's work had been seen in every one of London's available 'public' theatres – those open-air houses, where the groundlings stood around a raised thrust stage on three sides, while the enclosing tiers of galleries provided seating (and some protection from the elements) for patrons with an extra penny or two to spare.

Jonson's earliest hackwork in the 1590s was for Philip Henslowe, the canny impresario who at that time was running the Rose Theatre on Bankside with the Lord Admiral's Men. In 1597 Jonson had a hand in the revision of *The Isle of Dogs* at the nearby Swan, while the earliest play he himself acknowledged and preserved, *Every Man in His Humour*, was written in 1598 for the long-standing rivals to the Admiral's, the Lord Chamberlain's Men. At that time the Chamberlain's, the company to which Shakespeare belonged, were playing in London's northern 'theatre district' of Shoreditch, first at the original Theatre and then at the Curtain; but in 1599 they moved south of the river to the newly-built Globe, where Jonson's *Every Man out of His Humour* was one of the first plays to be performed. Later his *Bartholomew Fair* was among the earliest productions at the Hope, opened in 1614 and the last outdoor playhouse to be built in London.

In between, two other of the comic masterpieces of Jonson's vintage period, *Volpone* (1606) and *The Alchemist* (1610), had also been played at the Globe. But his satirical contributions to the 'war of the theatres' at the turn of the century were, like his 'regular' comedy of 1609, *Epicoene, or The Silent Woman*, played by companies of young boys – whose intermittent popularity had caused the players in *Hamlet* to go abroad in search of audiences. The children performed in playhouses quite different from those of the adult actors – the 'private', or indoor theatres, where higher admission charges and a considerably smaller capacity combined to produce a more socially-select audience. Here, the more fashionable spectators preferred to sit in the so-called pit area fronting the end-on stage – or, like Fitzdottrel, to show themselves off along the edge of the stage itself.

Thanks to their origins as royal choir-schools, these theatres had been able to evade the prohibition upon acting within the City of London. It was in hope of surmounting this ban that the Chamberlain's Men had leased and converted a suitable playing space within the former monastery of Blackfriars in 1596: but it was not until some time after 1609, when the theatres had been closed on account of the plague, that they were at last permitted to play there. It was at the Blackfriars that the King's Men (as the Chamberlain's became known when James himself became their patron) gave *The Devil is an Ass* its first performance, probably in the late autumn of 1616.

New theatres intended for the adult companies were subsequently built on similar lines, and both the Phoenix, converted from a cockpit in Drury Lane in 1616, and the Salisbury Court, opened in 1629, were indoor houses – establishing the pattern of theatre building as it continued to evolve after the Restoration. But both boy and adult players also performed in what was, in effect, London's 'third theatre', the court of King James, where Jonson was also active in 1616 – the year in which his old associates Henslowe and Shakespeare died, and one which was to prove in many ways a watershed in his own career.

A Watershed Year for Ben

The New Year of 1616 found King James's erstwhile favourite, Somerset, in disgrace. His wife had just been convicted of the murder of Sir Thomas Overbury, after a trial which brought to light a side of Jacobean life as seamy as any ever portrayed by Jonson. David Riggs's recent biography of Jonson includes 'pimps, apothecaries, assassins-for-hire, quack physicians, and corruptible officers' among those involved in the crime: and even the murder weapon had the bizarre quality of Jonson in scatological vein – a poisoned enema.

The clique surrounding George Villiers at court was now busily supplanting Somerset's men, and Ben's court masque for Twelfth Night 1616 celebrated the new order. Early in his masque-writing career Jonson had developed the 'anti-masque', played by professional actors, as a comic counterpoint to the stately music and song of the masque proper, with its dancers from the courtly elite. Here, the anti-masque concerned the alchemical manufacture of artificial humans – a motif probably suggested by the display at the Overbury trial of copulating lead figures, allegedly the work of the dead conjurer and avid playgoer Simon Forman. Spectators at the trial had feared that a loud creaking of the courtroom's ceiling rafters signified the Devil's fury at the discovery of his handiwork: and this event would still have been fresh in the audience's memory when Jonson's Satan in *The Devil is an Ass* makes his noisily damaging departure from Newgate.

In the masque itself, Jonson contrasted with such apparitions the true capacity of his King to create 'new' life, ennobled through his favours. Within the month, James had taken the hint, and rewarded Jonson himself with a pension for life of sixty-six pounds a year. At the same time, a project which had been close to Jonson's heart for several years was approaching fruition – the publication of his *Works* in a collected folio volume. Although duly attributed to their original dates, all nine plays included had in fact been thoroughly revised by Jonson, to give the impression of a career coherent in its development and classical in its precedents. But this cultivated persona was misleading, for as he grew older the dramatist in his work for the regular stage drew ever more strongly on native models and on the popular tradition – as he was doing in *The Devil is an Ass* while his *Works* were still fresh on the bookstalls.

The Devil and the Dramatic Tradition

King James was very interested in witchcraft and demonology, though over the years his views had mellowed from the credulity evident in his printed tract on the subject of 1597 to a much healthier scepticism. This had been justified, as it happened, in the summer of 1616, when, during a royal progress through Leicester, James had personally intervened to expose a fraudulent case of 'possession', in time to save the lives of at least some of those accused – though nine alleged 'witches' had already been hanged, thanks to local magistrates as anxious to convict as Jonson's Eitherside. A similar ambivalence pervades the dramatic treatment of the Devil in late-Elizabethan and Jacobean drama – a treatment which, inescapably, refers back to the traditions of the medieval and early Tudor moral interludes, or morality plays. In these, personified forces of good and evil did battle for the soul of a man – whose symbolic status is clear from the names given to the title characters of such morality plays as *Everyman* and *Mankind*. In both, man falls but, through God's grace, wins forgiveness and redemption.

It was in consciousness of this tradition that Christopher Marlowe, around 1590, wrote *Doctor Faustus* – in structure still a morality play, but now a tragic one: for its hero is incapable of repentance, and so is eventually cast into Hell. Yet *Faustus* is very much a morality play of the modern age – not only in the self-fashioned individualism of its hero, but in Mephistophilis's reminder that Hell is not (as Faustus assumes) somewhere else, but all around us. This rebuke to the literal-minded is reminiscent of Pug's warning to Fitzdottrel against the 'popular error' that devils are invariably cloven-hoofed. Indeed, the devils in both plays assume a 'pleasing shape': Mephistophilis appears to Faustus in the blasphemous guise of a friar, while Pug takes on the discarded body of a recently-hanged but young and personable thief. However, while Faustus makes his contract with Mephistophilis for twenty-four years, Jonson's Satan (more respectful of the neo-classical unities) talks Pug down to a mere twenty-four hours.

Unlike *Faustus*, most 'devil plays' of the period were comedies – such as *The Merry Devil of Edmonton*, written in 1602, but still proclaimed in Jonson's Prologue as his audience's 'dear delight'. But there is no real contradiction between the contempt Jonson expresses in his collected

Works for plays containing 'fools and devils' and the presence in *The Devil is an Ass* of Pug, Iniquity and Satan. These demons hold no terrors such as struck the great Marlovian actor Alleyn when, so the story goes, he counted one devil too many during a performance of *Doctor Faustus*. Between the bad angels of the moralities and Milton's cosmic tragic hero in *Paradise Lost*, Jonson's Satan is the ageing leader of a troupe of strolling players from a Hell's mouth which is an old-fashioned theatrical property.

Like the speaker of the Prologue, Satan in the first scene (perhaps emerging through the stage trap) is, then, well aware that he is a character in a play – and he knows that the devilish tricks which frightened the audiences of the moralities would now appear drably outdated. He shares, too, the awareness of Jonson's spectators that Iniquity is not a theological but a theatrical vice – one of those minor devils, representing specific sins, a little of whose traditional complicity with audiences rubbed off onto Richard III and even Iago. The 'innocent' Pug may still take delight in old Iniquity's 'jigging rhymes', but his 'dear chief' knows that such doggerel couplets have become quaintly archaic. More aware of modern tastes, Satan has thus caught up with the blank verse popularised by Marlowe – in the opening line of the play even trimming his traditional medieval roar into a proper iambic pentameter of 'Ho, ho's.

One of the ironies of the play is that Fitzdottrel abandons his pretence of being possessed by a demon at the very moment of learning that for the past day he has possessed a demon in very truth. But while the self-deluding squire incorporates at least three 'vices' – Avarice, Ambition and Vanity – into his own character, Merecraft and Engine, as the modern counterparts of 'bad angels', work far more effectively on him than does Pug: for the temptations they offer are those of the emerging capitalist system itself.

Monopolists, Courtiers and the Crown

Subtle and Face in *The Alchemist* batten upon the deepest desires of their clients, and engage with them through the single device of their pseudo-alchemy: but in *The Devil is an Ass* Merecraft, Engine, and Everill tailor a whole range of bespoke fantasies – a grandiose piece of land reclamation for the squire, a handy little monopoly in novelty tableware for a lowlier supplicant. And, of course, while alchemy was already regarded by people of sense as no more than a quack science, even the canniest could find themselves caught up in 'projects' – and such schemes, promising a quick return for a minimal investment, have gone on tempting the greedy and the gullible ever since.

So 'projecting' in *The Devil is an Ass* is not just a plot device to fool Fitzdottrel, but close to the actuality of Jacobean London – a means of making money through being granted a monopoly in the production or supply of goods, or for some such dubious scheme as the infamous Alderman Cockayne's for the finishing of cloth. As for Merecraft, he combines the skills of the entrepreneur with those of the copywriter: thus, his tactics for promoting his scheme for toothpicks (IV, i) are not so very different from those of a modern advertising agency puffing some modern miracle of dental hygiene.

Plans to reclaim the Fens were, as projects went, far from fantastical – although generally any success for one landowner was at the expense of his poorer and less influential neighbours. Recently one of King James's fellow Scots had been given the royal blessing for such a project, and it was perhaps on account of this that James, according to Jonson (as reported by the poet Drummond), had 'desired him to conceal' this element of the play. What *was* concealed we now have no means of knowing: but Merecraft's persuasions were close enough to reality to remind audiences that such patents and monopolies were dependent upon obtaining the ear of the King. For the royal prerogative of granting monopolies had now, rather dubiously, been reclaimed, to cope with the profligate James's latest cashflow crisis: and, according to the historian Christopher Hill, over 700 such patents had been granted by 1621. They were to remain one of the chief causes of friction between Parliament and Crown.

The exploitation of monopolies depended on a subtle interplay between merchants – or such intermediaries as Merecraft – and the aristocracy whose patronage was needful to gain access to the court and the King. Less subtly, the needs of courtiers for ready money left their estates mortgaged to city usurers – or saw 'land marrying money', one of the impulses behind the social mobility of the period. Thus, Gilthead, as Gamini Salgado points out, is allowed to talk much sense about the relationship between wealthy, hard-working citizens and their indolent 'betters'. And even his cautious son reflects wryly on the modern wheel of fortune which, should it declass and elevate him as his father hopes, will only mortgage his heirs to freshly-minted Giltheads a few generations hence. His very name, Plutarchus, is double-edged, implying both the learning of the classical historian and 'plutarchy' as the now-prevailing rule of wealth.

Jacobean 'Character' and the New Individualism

Jonson and his fellow satirists had no sense of the potential for social change in Renaissance society: rather, they looked back to a golden age of civility, hospitality, and acknowledged obligation that had never in truth existed. But at least the hierarchical loyalties and duties of feudalism had been predicated upon a sense of community that early modern capitalism (not yet recognised as such) was well-advanced in casting off.

It was in the seventeenth century that the word 'individual' first came into currency, to define the new breed of self-dedicated creatures so relentlessly mocked in Jonson's plays. And, ironically, its first recorded sense in the *Oxford English Dictionary* as 'expressing self-identity' concerns devilish goings-on in the theatre – the instance being quoted from Prynne's *Histriomastix*, a tract of 1633 in which the puritanical author condemns those who 'sport themselves with those individual sins upon the stage, which the parties . . . are condoling now in Hell'.

The more precise modern sense of 'individual', meaning simply one person distinguished from another, is first recorded in 1605, and this reminds us how alien was such a perception of individuality – not only to medieval ideals of social interdependence, but to the ideal of classical literature and art of rendering what was *typical* in humanity, and so of ridiculing 'individual' eccentricities with such satirical contempt as Jonson's. Jacobean 'character writing' accordingly treated its subjects not as 'psychologically-rounded' but as types, to which all in that category – as it might be, 'actors' or 'parasites' or 'worthy bishops' or 'effeminate fools' – were expected to conform. And such 'truth to type' is not merely justifiable but essential to the 'comedy of humours' which Jonson made his own.

Comedy of Humours – or Situation Comedy?

The critic Ann Barton suggests that *The Devil is an Ass* might well have been called 'The Further Adventures of Subtle and Face', after Jonson's con-men in *The Alchemist*. And she and other critics have identified a wide range not only of character-types but of situations and plot-points which Jonson redeploys in this play. Some attribute this to his recent saturation in his earlier output while he was preparing and revising the *Works*. Although this may indeed have had a heightening effect, it is in the nature of Jonsonian comedy to ring the changes in this way – and the use of a limited range of situations and 'characters' is no more a defect in art than, in our own day, are the instantly identifiable personae created by stand-up comics or double-acts, or the recurrently recognisable settings of 'situation comedy' on television. Hancock, *Steptoe and Son*, *The Young Ones*, *Absolutely Fabulous*, to select a handful of favourites stretching back over four decades, have all depended upon a consistent setting and a fair share of 'humorous' eccentrics – while Jonson's sprinkling of outright zanies anticipate the surreal creations of *The Goon Show* or *Monty Python*.

But, by 1616, Jonson's early theory of a 'comedy of humours', as a type of comedy peopled by characters reduced to their distinctive affectations or obsessions, had been considerably modified by his practice – at least in so far as its proclaimed moral purpose, of mocking such people out of their follies, was concerned. Indeed, after *Volpone* in 1606 – its ending so virtuous as to seem dramatically inappropriate – Jonson's plays do not depict the triumph of morality as such, but rather the defeat of stupidity and dullness, and the triumph of wit.

Sometimes still, as in *Epicoene* (1609), a measure of punishment is doled out: but by the close of *Bartholomew Fair* (1614) all the characters join together in feasting, just as, at the end of *The Devil is an Ass*, the actors (or so Jonson's Epilogue proposes) are going to take the poet out to supper. Nobody in either play is to be punished for their sins, and those few (the most pretentious rather than the wickedest) who have in passing been humiliated are not much the worse for their experiences – or for that matter much affected by them at all.

It is true that Jonson – by contrast (as so often) with Shakespeare – seems unconcerned with showing characters *changing* under the

pressure of events; yet arguably he is the greater realist for acknow-
ledging that most people do *not* change, merely adjust their habitual
behaviour to changed circumstances. Thus Fitzdottrel appears to
undergo a kind of existential crisis, affirming his individuality with
the cry (ironically echoing Webster's Duchess of Malfi): 'I will be what
I am, Fabian Fitzdottrel.' But that is at the end of Act Four, when the
play might easily have ended: and it is part of the purpose of Act Five
to show that Fitzdottrel is indeed what he is – which is what he has
always been, true to his type as a self-opinionated dupe or 'gull'.

By this time in his life, Jonson's expansive humanity was both too
kindly and too knowledgable over-harshly to condemn humankind –
his own Londonkind least of all. Even his clear contempt for Tailbush
and Eitherside is tempered, as is that typically Jacobean male distaste
for cosmetics, when the 'Spanish lady' rolls their properties round her
tongue with as much rhetorical relish as does Sir Epicure Mammon
in *The Alchemist* the exotic ingredients of his recipes for decadent
delights.

Like Mammon's premonitions of the water-bed or the sunken bath,
some of Merecraft's projects have come close enough to being realised
for twentieth-century consumers, yet are here carried to heights of
absurdity by confidence man and victim alike. The idea of an 'Office
of Dependances', a sort of registry for intending duellists to ensure the
proper disposition of the loser's estate, displays a bureaucratic logic
which is irresistible – not least to Fitzdottrel, who wants to know every
last detail of how it works. And the closing scenes are replete with self-
contained comic turns: the attempt of Tailbush and Eitherside to
improve Pug's ancestry by pronouncing him De-vile; Pug's waning
fluency under the catechising of the ladies; Fitzdottrel's attempt to
evade his self-imposed 'dependency' by feigning demonic possession;
Ambler's initially hesitant, then unstoppable confession (not to men-
tion his filofax of male toiletries); and Pug's simulated deafness under
accusation, with its non-sequiturs of escalating irrelevance.

Women, Wooing, and a Freudian Footnote

It is an incidental reflection upon the use in the drama of 'aptronyms',
summing up characters through descriptive names, that wives and

daughters from Frances Fitzdottrel to Wycherley's Marjorie Pinchwife to Shaw's Eliza Doolittle have had to take on attributes of their men-folk which they do not themselves display. Here, though, Eitherside does nicely for wife as well as husband, suggesting a liking for both sexes no less than a capacity to argue both sides of a case. And we see no Lord Tailbush, so that name is all the lady's own – its sexual overtones quite as overt as all those Wishforts and Cockwoods of Restoration comedy half a century or so later.

In fleshing out the male-constructed dramatic typology of the female, Jonson had always been better at whores or viragos than virgins or virtuous wives. But by this stage of his career he was able to create in Frances a 'good' female character rather more attractive than the insipid Celia in *Volpone* or the cold-blooded Grace of *Bartholomew Fair* – both of whom, moreover, are *acted upon* by other characters rather than dramatically active. Frances Fitzdottrel has a mind as well as a body of her own.

In *Bartholomew Fair*, Jonson had bravely attacked the wardship system, whereby his own patron, the King, appointed guardians to orphaned heiresses, who could, in effect, then be sold off to the highest bidder. In *Devil*, his unexpected streak of feminism (or sense of natural justice) leads him to secure for Frances Fitzdottrel as much independence as her inescapable yoking to her dolt of a husband will allow. She and her foolish spouse function, indeed, as twin epicentres to the play's double-plot, and the tremors caused by Wittipol's wooing of Frances occasionally overlap with those caused by Fitzdottrel's deception – first and crucially in the matter of the cloak, later in Wittipol's disguise as the Spanish lady, which complicates matters still further by causing Fitzdottrel to fall in love with him.

So if, as some critics suggest, Jonson is here trying his hand at romantic comedy after the manner of Shakespeare, it is romance of a very odd kind. Its heroine is an inescapably married woman, and, as the scholar Peter Happé has pointed out, its hero Wittipol is put under some sort of constraint in all three of his big scenes – by the enforced silence of Frances and the presence of Fitzdottrel in the first, by the gulf between the supposed balconies in the second, and by his female disguise in the third.

Finally, that uncomfortable character Manly – poised half-way between the Good Angel of Wittipol's conscience and some sententious confidant from an eighteenth-century sentimental comedy – interposes himself at the crucial moment in Act Four, Scene Six, declaring that he has been keeping constant vigil over the couple in the cause of innocence. What can poor Wittipol do, caught as if between the morality play and the moral majority?

But Pug, too, has had his ironic role to play in preserving the sanctity of marriage – his first encouragement of Frances to adultery having a contrary effect, since she presumes it to be a typical, would-be devious ploy of her husband's to put her faithfulness to the test. When this earns Pug a beating, he revenges himself by betraying the assignation with Wittipol – who is thus largely thwarted in what proves to be his final chance to gear up his assault on Frances from the lyrical to the physical. Two kinds of horns are put out of commission in this play, the cuckold's no less than the devil's.

Jonson had been separated for long periods from his own wife, and seductions interrupted by enraged husbands had become a recurrent motif in his plays, reflecting who knows what actualities or guilts in his own confessed adulteries. In this sense, perhaps Freud would have seen Pug's instinctual sex drive as an expression of the dramatist's Id, ineffectually contesting matters with the more socialised Ego of Wittipol and the superhuman Super-Ego which is Manly. We might in this way begin at least to see that our own simplifications are no less true and no less trite than those of a medieval morality, and even understand if not resolve our play's structural oddities and moral ambivalence: what we cannot do is make of it a romantic comedy.

'Modes of Perception'

As Anne Barton points out, the friendship of the two gallants of *The Devil is an Ass*, Wittipol and Manly, is no less equivocal than that of the young gentlemen of *Epicene* or of Winwife and Quarlous in *Bartholomew Fair*. This she takes as betraying 'an underlying lack of trust' which pervades the whole play. She points out that the word 'trust' and its variants occur 'no fewer than thirty times' in *The Devil is an Ass* – while Richard Allen Cave trumps this by accumulating some sixty references to precise sums of money (a more pertinent reckoning, I think, in a play whose characters are much concerned with putting a price on everything yet who know the value of nothing).

But here William Empson's admission in his famous essay on the multiple meanings of the word 'honesty' in *Othello* is instructive: for he acknowledges that when he first saw Shakespeare's tragedy on stage he had not noticed the recurrence at all. And word-counts are of even less help to actors than the image-clusters once so popular with literary critics when it comes to *playing* the concepts they evoke – particularly one tossed around between so many different characters as 'trust' is here. If anything, its repetition only affirms the slipperiness of its meaning, along the semantic spectrum between minor devils *trusted* to win souls for a Satanic master, confidence tricksters winning misplaced *trust*, and hopeful lovers soliciting the *trust* of would-be mistresses. Perhaps Jonson's concern, if the frequency of use is more than accidental, was to suggest that, like the ubiquitous 'excellence' today, 'trust' was a 'weasel word', used to conceal rather than reveal meaning.

Cave, indeed, gets closer to the feeling of the play on stage when he declares that Jonson's subject is 'dramatic conventions, and what they imply about an audience's moral scruples and modes of perception'. For it is true that from the moment when the speaker of the Prologue comes on to 'clear a space' among the fashionable attention-seekers – permitted to sit along the sides of the stage in the indoor theatres – and Jonson proceeds in his opening scene to show us devils straight out of the old moralities, we can be left in little doubt that we are in a theatre, watching actors perform a play, not being lulled into what the romantics were later to call 'suspension of disbelief'.

It is perhaps Fitzdottrel who most fully occupies the parallel time shared by the play and its audience – itself an ironic use of the neoclassical 'verisimilitude' which Jonson observes in this dimension, though he cheerfully ignores the other 'unities', of place and action. Fitzdottrel is as anxious to avoid the cuckolding his own greed almost brings about as he is to acquire the dukedom promised by Merecraft: yet he is concerned, too, that none of this should prevent him getting to the Blackfriars theatre on time – for the start of the new play, which is called *The Devil is an Ass*. Once there, he is accustomed, we gather, to sit on the side of the stage, where today he plans to show off his new cloak – and to get in the way of the actors, as the Prologue anticipates. Even the prospect of leaving after one act does not disturb him, since it will clearly disturb others – and thus draw attention to himself and his cloak. In this way Fitzdottrel is 'observed' as both a character in a play and a member of its audience: and maybe the audience will observe aspects of themselves in him.

Later, Merecraft points out that if the erstwhile boy-actor and consummate female impersonator Dick Robinson is hired to play the 'Spanish lady', he is liable to gossip to the poets – and they will all be in danger of being made into . . . characters in a play. In the event, of course, it is Wittipol who takes on the role – but there is at least a high probability that the actor of the King's company who played Wittipol was the now-adult Dick Robinson (his height, like Wittipol's, a reminder of the impersonation). So Robinson, playing Wittipol, was 'playing' a part for which, within the play, he had just been rejected by Merecraft and Engine. However, the questions thus raised for me by the audience's 'metatheatrical' awareness of sharing the play with the actors have less to do with what Cave calls their 'moral scruples' than with their 'modes of perception' – prompting a consideration of that most elusive of a play's qualities, the 'language' of its performance.

Jonson in Performance

Why, after the flexibility of prose which Jonson so fully and richly exploited in *Bartholomew Fair*, did he return in *The Devil is an Ass* to the disciplines of blank verse? A little earlier, he had written *Epicoene* in prose followed by *The Alchemist* in verse, so it was not a matter of a growing conviction of the superiority of one mode over the other. Nor does he follow the 'decorum' observed by Shakespeare, of using prose for common characters and verse for the nobility. Indeed, he is not much concerned with the nobility – for, as Peter Barnes, a dramatist with unmatched experienced in adapting Jonson for the modern stage, reminds us: 'Shakespeare gives us rulers, Jonson the ruled.' It is vital in production, Barnes goes on, 'to remember that the majority of his characters are workers' – and giving verse dialogue to those workers makes them 'work' to quite a different rhythm than Shakespeare's.

When characters in Shakespearean comedy argue, they do so in a way which suggests they are listening and responding to their opponents; other conversations, too, proceed with the inner logic of careful attention being paid. But Jonson's characters are as often as not oblivious to what everybody else is saying – beyond waiting to pounce on some cue which will permit them to plunge in with their own flood of words. Generally, they already know what they are going to say – and when they do not, you can feel them feeling for the words. In prose, this makes for a sharp, colloquial realism: in verse, it makes for the felt artifice, the rhetorical bounce, of dialogue disciplined and energised as the 'line' of verse helps also to shape the 'line' of comic intention.

This is especially evident in all the run-on and split lines which set up constant currents and eddies of actorly exchange – and also require full attention to be paid to the other stage 'languages', of gesture and spatial interaction. Thus, as Barnes claims, Jonson's characters tend to 'enter full blast. There is no build-up. They gallop on flogging their favourite hobby-horse.' All is forward movement, and there is little time for reflections on the past: 'There are no yesterdays in Jonson, only todays and uncertain tomorrows.' Thus, the sub-text 'is always on the surface': whatever deceits and subterfuges are going on, we know all about them and the motives which underpin them – these being driven (again by contrast with Shakespearean comedy) less often by the sexual impulse than by imperatives of money and ambition.

Although we know nothing of the stage history, if any, of *The Devil is an Ass* after its first performance in 1616, Peter Barnes has brought it firmly back into the modern repertoire – his version having first been played at the Nottingham Playhouse in 1970, then, six years later, in a production by the Birmingham Repertory company which toured to the Edinburgh Festival. Barnes's second revival was seen briefly in London in 1977, and he has also adapted the play for BBC Radio 3. The Royal Shakespeare Company mounted its own first production of the play at the Swan Theatre in Stratford in the Spring of 1995.

A Note on the Text

Perhaps because of King James's displeasure with Jonson's handling of the projecting theme, *The Devil is an Ass* did not appear in print until

1631, by which time Jonson, incapacitated by a stroke, is unlikely to have been able to supervise its preparation as closely as he did that of his *Works*. This is, none the less, the only authoritative text, and our edition is based upon it. (It was originally prepared by Peter Happé for the 'Revels Plays' series in 1994.) Here, Jonson's spelling and, more cautiously, his punctuation have been modernised – but original usages have been retained where these offer guidance to pronunciation or stress. Thus, Jonson's distinctive marking of elisions is retained – *he'has*, for example, as distinct from our modern *he's* or *he has*.

It will also be observed that a 'scene' in Jonson is quite unlike a scene in a Shakespearean text, whose end is marked by a complete clearance of the stage. Jonson follows the neoclassical convention of marking a new scene when a major change occurs in the composition of the characters – and this is entirely appropriate to his own manner of constructing units of action, which often resemble comic sketches – sometimes stand-up turns or double-acts – rather than stages in the advancement of plot or character-relationships. As always in Jonson's version of neoclassicism, the form is there to serve the substance.

Simon Trussler

For Further Reading

Two recent works which provide helpful (and helpfully contrasting) guides through Jonson's work on a play-by-play basis are Anne Barton's *Ben Jonson, Dramatist* (Cambridge UP, 1984) and Richard Allen Cave's *Ben Jonson* (Macmillan, 1991), while Peter Womack's *Ben Jonson* (Oxford: Blackwell, 1986) considers the work illuminatingly from various conceptual standpoints. Rosalind Miles's *Ben Jonson: His Life and Work* (London: Routledge, 1986) and David Riggs's *Ben Jonson: a Life* (Cambridge, Mass: Harvard UP, 1989) both offer critical analyses of the plays within the context of the writer's life. Older works which remain of value include L. C. Knights's *Drama and Society in the Age of Jonson* (London: Chatto, 1937), Edward B. Partridge's *The Broken Compass: a Study of the Major Comedies of Ben Jonson* (London: Chatto, 1958), and Jonas A. Barish's *Ben Jonson and the Language of Prose Comedy* (Cambridge, Mass: Harvard UP, 1960).

Collections of essays find *The Devil is an Ass* poorly represented, but *Ben Jonson* in the 'Twentieth Century Views' series, edited by Jonas A. Barish, contains some seminal criticism from earlier in the century, including the now widely challenged views of T. S. Eliot, Harry Levin, and Edmund Wilson. Peter Barnes's essay on 'Staging Jonson' is to be found in *Jonson and Shakespeare*, edited by Ian Donaldson (Atlantic Highlands, NJ: Humanities Press, 1983), while a special issue of the magazine *Gambit* (No. 22, 1974) struck a rare balance between academic and theatrical contributors.

Useful background reading on the theatrical context includes Andrew Gurr's masterly conspective survey of *The Shakespearean Stage* (Cambridge UP, 1970), Keith Sturgess's *Jacobean Private Theatre* (London: Routledge, 1987), and G. E. Bentley's *The Profession of Dramatist in Shakespeare's Time* (Princeton UP, 1971).

Jonson: Key Dates

1572   Born, 11 June. 'Brought up poorly' in his early childhood.

1583   *c.* Educated at Westminster School until *c.* 1588.

1591   *c.* Volunteered to fight for the Dutch in Flanders.

1594   Married Anne Lewis – 'a shrew yet honest'.

1597   Became an actor and jobbing playwright in London under the manager Philip Henslowe. August-October, imprisoned for his share in the 'lewd' and 'seditious' lost comedy *The Isle of Dogs.*

1598   *The Case is Altered* performed by the Children of the Chapel. First success with *Every Man in His Humour* for the Lord Chamberlain's Men. Killed Gabriel Spencer, a fellow actor, in a duel, for which he was imprisoned (pleading 'benefit of clergy') and his goods confiscated. Became a Catholic in prison.

1599   Collaborated with Dekker and others on the lost tragedies *Page of Plymouth* and *Robert II, King of Scots. Every Man out of His Humour* played by the Lord Chamberlain's Men.

1600   The 'war of the theatres', to which Jonson contributed *Cynthia's Revels* and *Poetaster*, both for the Chapel Children.

1601   Revisions to Kyd's *The Spanish Tragedy* for Henslowe.

1602   Separation of five years from his wife.

1603   Accession of James I. Jonson wrote his first royal entertainment, the *King's Entertainment at Althorp*, but was also called before the Privy Council to answer for suspected papist tendencies in *Sejanus*, his unsuccessful tragedy for the King's Men.

1605   His first masque, *The Masque of Blackness*, performed at court, but his collaboration with Marston and Chapman on *Eastward Ho!* (played by the Queen's Revels at Blackfriars) landed him again in prison. Minor involvement in Gunpowder Plot.

1606   The masque *Hymenaei* performed at court, *Volpone* at the Globe.

1609   *Epicoene* played by the Children of Whitefriars.

1610   *The Alchemist* played by the King's Men. About this time Jonson
       returned to the Anglican faith.

1611   Second and last tragedy, *Catiline*, also a failure. Throughout this
       period writing masques and entertainments, this year's being
       The Masque of Oberon and *Love Freed from Ignorance and Folly*.

1612   Travelled to France as tutor to son of Sir Walter Raleigh.

1614   Lady Elizabeth's Men staged *Bartholomew Fair* at the Hope.

1616   Granted annual pension of one hundred marks by the king.
       Published his *Works* in folio. Performance of *The Devil is an Ass*
       by the King's Men at the Blackfriars, after which Jonson
       devoted his energies for next ten years to writing for the court.

1619   Made honorary Master of Arts by Oxford University.

1623   Fire in Jonson's lodgings destroyed his books and manuscripts.
       Contributed a verse tribute to the First Folio of Shakespeare's
       collected plays.

1626   First of Jonson's final group of comedies, *The Staple of News*.

1628   Confined to his chambers by a paralytic stroke.

1632   *The Magnetic Lady*, probably his last comedy, played by the
       King's Men.

1637   Died on 6 August, and buried in Westminster Abbey.

THE DEVIL IS AN ASS

The Persons of the Play

SATAN.	The great Devil.	
PUG.	The less Devil.	
INIQUITY.	The Vice.	
FITZDOTTREL.	A Squire of Norfolk.	
MISTRESS FRANCES.	His wife.	5
MERECRAFT.	The Projector.	
EVERILL.	His Champion.	
WITTIPOL.	A young Gallant.	
MANLY.	His friend.	
ENGINE.	A Broker.	10
TRAINS.	The Projector's man.	
GILTHEAD.	A Goldsmith.	
PLUTARCHUS.	His son.	
SIR PAUL EITHERSIDE.	A Lawyer, and Justice.	
LADY EITHERSIDE.	His wife.	15
LADY TAILBUSH.	The Lady Projectress.	
PITFALL.	Her woman.	
AMBLER.	Her Gentleman Usher.	
SLEDGE.	A Smith, the Constable.	
SHACKLES.	Keeper of Newgate.	20
SERGEANTS.		
[THE PROLOGUE.]		
[THE EPILOGUE.]		
[FOUR KEEPERS at Newgate.]		
[WAITERS.]		25

The scene, London.

The Prologue

'The Devil is an Ass.' That is today
The name of what you are met for, a new play.
Yet, grandees, would you were not come to grace
Our matter with allowing us no place.
Though you presume Satan a subtle thing,   5
And may have heard he's worn in a thumb-ring,
Do not on these presumptions, force us act
In compass of a cheese-trencher. This tract
Will ne'er admit our vice, because of yours.
Anon, who, worse than you, the fault endures   10
That yourselves make, when you will thrust and spurn,
And knock us o' the elbows, and bid, turn;
As if, when we had spoke, we must be gone,
Or, till we speak, must all run in to one,
Like the young adders at the old one's mouth?   15
Would we could stand due north; or had no south,
If that offend: or were Muscovy glass,
That you might look our scenes through as they pass.
We know not how to affect you. If you'll come
To see new plays, pray you afford us room,   20
And show this but the same face you have done
Your dear delight, 'The Devil of Edmonton'.
Or if, for want of room, it must miscarry,
'Twill be but justice that your censure tarry
Till you give some. And when six times you ha' seen't,   25
If this play do not like, the devil is in't.

Act I, Scene i

[*Enter* SATAN *and*] PUG.

[SATAN.] Ho, ho, ho, ho, ho, ho, ho, ho, etc.
To earth? And why to earth, thou foolish spirit?
What wouldst thou do on earth?

PUG.   For that, great chief,
As time shall work. I do but ask my month,
Which every petty puisne devil has;   5
Within that term the Court of Hell will hear
Something may gain a longer grant perhaps.

SATAN. For what? The laming a poor cow or two?
Entering a sow to make her cast her farrow?
Or crossing of a market-woman's mare   10
'Twixt this and Tottenham? These were wont to be
Your main achievements, Pug. You have some plot now
Upon a tunning of ale, to stale the yeast,
Or keep the churn so that the butter come not
Spite o' the housewife's cord or her hot spit?   15
Or some good ribibe about Kentish Town,
Or Hoxton, you would hang now for a witch,
Because she will not let you play round Robin?
And you'll go sour the citizens' cream 'gainst Sunday:
That she may be accused for't, and condemned   20
By a Middlesex jury, to the satisfaction
Of their offended friends, the Londoners' wives,
Whose teeth were set on edge with it? Foolish fiend,
Stay i' your place, know your own strengths, and put not
Beyond the sphere of your activity.   25
You are too dull a devil to be trusted
Forth in those parts, Pug, upon any affair
That may concern our name on earth. It is not

Everyone's work. The state of Hell must care
Whom it employs in point of reputation, 30
Here about London. You would make, I think,
An agent to be sent, for Lancashire
Proper enough; or some parts of Northumberland,
So you'd good instructions, Pug.

PUG.   O chief!
You do not know, dear chief, what there is in me. 35
Prove me but for a fortnight, for a week,
And lend me but a Vice to carry with me,
To practise there, with any playfellow,
And you will see there will come more upon't,
Than you'll imagine, precious chief.

SATAN.   What Vice? 40
What kind wouldst thou'have it of?

PUG.   Why any – Fraud,
Or Covetousness, or Lady Vanity,
Or old Iniquity: I'll call him hither.

[*Enter* INIQUITY.]

INIQUITY. What is he calls upon me and would seem to lack a Vice?
Ere his words be half spoken, I am with him in a trice; 45
Here, there, and everywhere, as the cat is with the mice:
True *vetus Iniquitas*. Lack'st thou cards, friend, or dice?
I will teach thee to cheat, child, to cog, lie, and swagger,
And ever and anon to be drawing forth thy dagger:
To swear by Gog's nowns like a Lusty Juventus, 50
In a cloak to thy heel, and a hat like a penthouse,
Thy breeches of three fingers, and thy doublet all belly,
With a wench that shall feed thee with cock-stones and jelly.

PUG. Is it not excellent, chief? How nimble he is!

INIQUITY. Child of hell, this is nothing! I will fetch thee a leap 55
From the top of Paul's steeple to the Standard in Cheap:
And lead thee a dance through the streets without fail,
Like a needle of Spain, with a thread at my tail.
We will survey the suburbs, and make forth our sallies

Down Petticoat Lane, and up the Smock Alleys,   60
To Shoreditch, Whitechapel, and so to Saint Katharine's,
To drink with the Dutch there, and take forth their patterns.
From thence we will put in at Custom House Quay there,
And see how the factors and prentices play there
False with their masters; and geld many a full pack,   65
To spend it in pies at the Dagger, and the Woolsack.

PUG. Brave, brave, Iniquity! Will not this do, chief?

INIQUITY. Nay, boy, I will bring thee to the bawds and the roisters,
    At Billingsgate, feasting with claret wine, and oysters,   69
    From thence shoot the bridge, child, to the Cranes i' the Vintry,
    And see there the gimlets, how they make their entry!
    Or if thou hadst rather, to the Strand down to fall
    'Gainst the lawyers come dabbled from Westminster Hall,
    And mark how they cling with their clients together,
    Like ivy to oak, so velvet to leather –   75
    Ha, boy, I would show thee!

PUG.   Rare, rare!

SATAN.   Peace, dotard.
    And thou more ignorant thing, that so admir'st,
    Art thou the spirit thou seem'st? So poor? To choose
    This for a Vice t'advance the cause of Hell
    Now? As vice stands this present year? Remember,   80
    What number it is. Six hundred and sixteen.
    Had it but been five hundred, though some sixty
    Above – that's fifty years agone, and six,
    When every great man had his Vice stand by him,
    In his long coat, shaking his wooden dagger –   85
    I could consent that then this your grave choice
    Might have done that, with his lord chief, the which
    Most of his chamber can do now. But Pug,
    As the times are, who is it will receive you?
    What company will you go to? Or whom mix with?   90
    Where canst thou carry him? Except to taverns?
    To mount up on a joint-stool with a Jew's trump,
    To put down Cokeley, and that must be to citizens?

He ne'er will be admitted there where Vennor comes.
He may perchance, in tail of a sheriff's dinner,   95
Skip with a rhyme o' the table from new nothing,
And take his almain leap into a custard,
Shall make my Lady Mayoress and her sisters
Laugh all their hoods over their shoulders. But
This is not that will do; they are other things   100
That are received now upon earth for Vices,
Stranger, and newer: and changed every hour.
They ride 'em like their horses off their legs,
And here they come to Hell, whole legions of 'em,
Every week, tired. We still strive to breed   105
And rear 'em up new ones; but they do not stand
When they come there: they turn 'em on our hands.
And it is feared they have a stud o' their own
Will put down ours. Both our breed and trade
Will suddenly decay, if we prevent not.   110
Unless it be a Vice of quality
Or fashion now, they take none from us. Car-men
Are got into the yellow starch, and chimney-sweepers
To their tobacco and strong waters, hum,
Mead, and obarm. We must therefore aim   115
At extraordinary subtle ones now,
When we do send, to keep us up in credit,
Not old Iniquities. Get you e'en back, sir,
To making of your rope of sand again.
You are not for the manners, nor the times: 120
They have their Vices there most like to Virtues;
You cannot know 'em apart by any difference:
They wear the same clothes, eat the same meat,
Sleep i' the selfsame beds, ride i' those coaches,
Or very like, four horses in a coach,   125
As the best men and women. Tissue gowns,
Garters and roses, fourscore pound a pair,
Embroidered stockings, cut-work smocks, and shirts,
More certain marks of lechery now, and pride,
Than e'er they were of true nobility!   130

[Exit INIQUITY.]

But Pug, since you do burn with such desire
To do the commonwealth of Hell some service
I am content, assuming of a body
You go to earth, and visit men a day.
But you must take a body ready-made, Pug,   135
I can create you none: nor shall you form
Yourself an airy one, but become subject
To all impression of the flesh you take
So far as human frailty. So this morning
There is a handsome cutpurse hanged at Tyburn,   140
Whose spirit departed, you may enter his body:
For clothes employ your credit with the hangman,
Or let our tribe of brokers furnish you.
And look how far your subtlety can work
Through those organs; with that body, spy   145
Amongst mankind. You cannot there want vices,
And therefore the less need to carry 'em wi' you.
But as you make your soon at night's relation,
And we shall find it merits from the state,
You shall have both trust from us and employment.   150

PUG. Most gracious chief!

SATAN.   Only thus more I bind you
To serve the first man that you meet; and him
I'll show you now: observe him.

He shows FITZDOTTREL *to him, coming forth.*

                    Yon is he,
You shall see first, after your clothing. Follow him:
But once engaged, there you must stay and fix;   155
Not shift until the midnight's cock do crow.

PUG. Any conditions to be gone.

SATAN.   Away, then.

   [*Exeunt.*]

Act I, Scene ii

[*Enter*] FITZDOTTREL.

[FITZDOTTREL.] Ay they do now name Bretnor, as before
    They talked of Gresham, and of Doctor Forman,
    Franklin, and Fiske, and Savory – he was in too –
    But there's not one of these that ever could
    Yet show a man the Devil in true sort.   5
    They have their crystals, I do know, and rings,
    And virgin parchment, and their dead men's skulls,
    Their ravens' wings, their lights, and pentacles
    With characters; I ha'seen all these. But –
    Would I might see the Devil. I would give   10
    A hundred o' these pictures, so to see him
    Once out of picture. May I prove a cuckold,
    And that's the one main mortal thing I fear,
    If I begin not now to think the painters
    Have only made him. 'Slight, he would be seen   15
    One time or other else. He would not let
    An ancient gentleman of a good house
    As most are now in England, the Fitzdottrels,
    Run wild and call upon him thus in vain,
    As I ha' done this twelvemonth. If he be not   20
    At all, why are there conjurers? If they be not,
    Why are there laws against 'em? The best artists
    Of Cambridge, Oxford, Middlesex, and London,
    Essex, and Kent, I have had in pay to raise him
    These fifty weeks, and yet he'appears not. 'Sdeath,   25
    I shall suspect they can make circles only
    Shortly, and know but his hard names. They do say
    He'll meet a man of himself, that has a mind to him.
    If he would do so, I have a mind and a half for him:
    He should not be long absent. Pray thee, come,   30
    I long for thee. An' I were with child by him,
    And my wife too, I could not more.

He expresses a longing to see the Devil.

                      Come yet,

Good Beelzebub. Were he a kind devil,
And had humanity in him, he would come but
To save one's longing. I should use him well,   35
I swear, and with respect – would he would try me –
Not as the conjurers do when they ha' raised him;
Get him in bonds, and send him post, on errands
A thousand miles; it is preposterous, that,
And, I believe, is the true cause he comes not.   40
And he has reason. Who would be engaged
That might live freely as he may do? I swear
They are wrong all. The burnt child dreads the fire.
They do not know to entertain the Devil.
I would so welcome him, observe his diet,   45
Get him his chamber hung with arras – two of 'em –
I' my own house; lend him my wife's wrought pillows:
And as I am an honest man, I think,
If he had a mind to her too, I should grant him
To make our friendship perfect. So I would not   50
To every man. If he but hear me now!
And should come to me in a brave young shape,
And take me at my word! Ha! Who is this?

Act I, Scene iii

[*Enter*] PUG.

[PUG.] Sir, your good pardon that I thus presume
  Upon your privacy. I am born a gentleman,
  A younger brother; but in some disgrace
  Now with my friends: and want some little means
  To keep me upright, while things be reconciled.   5
  Please you, to let my service be of use to you, sir.

FITZDOTTREL. Service? 'Fore hell, my heart was at my mouth,
  Till I had viewed his shoes well, for those roses
  Were big enough to hide a cloven foot.

He looks and surveys his feet, over and over.

No, friend, my number's full. I have one servant,   10
Who is my all, indeed; and from the broom
Unto the brush: for just so far, I trust him.
He is my wardrobe man, my cater, cook,
Butler, and steward; looks unto my horse;
And helps to watch my wife. He has all the places   15
That I can think on, from the garret downward
E'en to the manger, and the curry-comb.

PUG. Sir, I shall put your worship to no charge
More than my meat, and that but very little;
I'll serve you for your love.

FITZDOTTREL.   Ha? Without wages?   20
I'd harken o' that ear were I at leisure.
But now I'm busy. Prithee, friend, forbear me;
And'thou hadst been a devil, I should say
Somewhat more to thee. Thou dost hinder, now,
My meditations.

PUG.   Sir, I am a devil.   25

FITZDOTTREL. How!

PUG.   A true devil, sir;

FITZDOTTREL.   Nay, now you lie –
Under your favour, friend, for I'll not quarrel.
I looked o' your feet afore; you cannot cozen me,
Your shoe's not cloven, sir, you are whole hoofed.

He views his feet again.

PUG. Sir, that's a popular error deceives many: 30
But I am that I tell you.

FITZDOTTREL.   What's your name?

PUG. My name is Devil, sir.

FITZDOTTREL.   Sayest thou true?

PUG.   Indeed, sir.

FITZDOTTREL. 'Slid! There's some omen i'this. What countryman?

PUG. Of Derbyshire, sir, about the Peak.

FITZDOTTREL.   That hole
  Belonged to your ancestors?

PUG. Yes, Devil's Arse, sir.   35

FITZDOTTREL. I'll entertain him for the name sake. Ha?
  And turn away my tother man? And save
  Four pound a year by that! There's luck, and thrift too!
  The very Devil may come hereafter as well.
  Friend, I receive you: but withal I acquaint you   40
  Aforehand, if you' offend me I must beat you.
  It is a kind of exercise I use,
  And cannot be without.

PUG.   Yes, if I do not
  Offend, you can, sure.

FITZDOTTREL. Faith, Devil, very hardly: 45
  I'll call you by your surname, 'cause I love it.

Act I, Scene iv

[*Enter*] ENGINE, WITTIPOL, [*and*] MANLY.

[ENGINE.] Yonder he walks, sir. I'll go lift him for you.

WITTIPOL. To him, good Engine, raise him up by degrees
  Gently, and hold him there too; you can do it.
  Show yourself now a mathematical broker.

ENGINE. I'll warrant you for half a piece.

WITTIPOL.   'Tis done, sir.   5

  [ENGINE *and* FITZDOTTREL *walk aside*.]

MANLY. Is't possible there should be such a man?

WITTIPOL. You shall be your own witness; I'll not labour
   To tempt you past your faith.

MANLY.   And is his wife
   So very handsome, say you?

WITTIPOL.   I ha' not seen her
   Since I came home from travel: and they say   10
   She is not altered. Then, before I went,
   I saw her once; but so as she hath stuck
   Still i' my view, no object hath removed her.

MANLY. 'Tis a fair guest, friend, beauty: and once lodged
   Deep in the eyes, she hardly leaves the inn.   15
   How does he keep her?

WITTIPOL.   Very brave. However
   Himself be sordid, he is sensual that way.
   In every dressing he does study her.

MANLY. And furnish forth himself so from the brokers?

WITTIPOL. Yes, that's a hired suit he now has on,   20
   To see 'The Devil is an Ass' today in:
   This Engine gets three or four pound a week by him.
   He dares not miss a new play, or a feast,
   What rate soever clothes be at; and thinks
   Himself still new, in other men's old.

MANLY.   But stay,   25
   Does he love meat so?

WITTIPOL.   Faith he does not hate it.
   But that's not it. His belly and his palate
   Would be compounded with for reason. Marry,
   A wit he has of that strange credit with him
   'Gainst all mankind; as it doth make him do   30
   Just what it list. It ravishes him forth,
   Whither it please, to any assembly' or place,
   And would conclude him ruined, should he scape
   One public meeting, out of the belief
   He has of his own great and catholic strengths   35

In arguing, and discourse.

ENGINE *hath won* FITZDOTTREL *to 'say on the cloak.*

It takes, I see:
He'has got the cloak upon him.

FITZDOTTREL.   A fair garment,
By my faith, Engine!

ENGINE.   It was never made, sir,
For threescore pound, I assure you: 'twill yield thirty.
The plush, sir, cost three pound ten shillings a yard!   40
And then the lace and velvet.

FITZDOTTREL.   I shall, Engine,
Be looked at prettily in it! Art thou sure
The play is played today?

ENGINE.   O here's the bill, sir.
I'd forgot to gi't you.

FITZDOTTREL.   Ha? 'The Devil!'

He gives him the playbill.

I will not lose you, sirrah! But, Engine, think you,   45
The gallant is so furious in his folly?
So mad upon the matter that he'll part
With's cloak upo' these terms?

ENGINE.   Trust not your Engine,
Break me to pieces else, as you would do
A rotten crane, or an old rusty jack,   50
That has not one true wheel in him. Do but talk with him.

FITZDOTTREL. I shall do that to satisfy you, Engine,
And myself too.

He turns to WITTIPOL.

With your leave, gentlemen.
Which of you is it, is so mere idolater
To my wife's beauty, and so very prodigal   55
Unto my patience, that for the short parley

Of one swift hour's quarter with my wife
He will depart with – let me see – this cloak here,
The price of folly? Sir, are you the man?

WITTIPOL. I am that venturer, sir.

FITZDOTTREL.   Good time! Your name   60
Is Wittipol?

WITTIPOL.   The Same, sir.

FITZDOTTREL.   And 'tis told me
You've travelled lately?

WITTIPOL.   That I have, sir.

FITZDOTTREL.   Truly,
Your travels may have altered your complexion;
But sure, your wit stood still.

WITTIPOL.   It may well be, sir.
All heads ha'not like growth.

FITZDOTTREL.   The good man's gravity   65
That left you land, your father, never taught you
These pleasant matches?

WITTIPOL.   No, nor can his mirth,
With whom I make 'em, put me off.

FITZDOTTREL.   You are
Resolved then?

WITTIPOL.   Yes, sir.

FITZDOTTREL.   Beauty is the saint
You'll sacrifice yourself into the shirt to?   70

WITTIPOL. So I may still clothe, and keep warm your wisdom?

FITZDOTTREL. You lade me, sir!

WITTIPOL.   I know what you will bear, sir.

FITZDOTTREL. Well, to the point. 'Tis only, sir, you say,
To speak unto my wife?

WITTIPOL.   Only to speak to her.

FITZDOTTREL. And in my presence?

WITTIPOL.   In your very presence.   75

FITZDOTTREL. And in my hearing?

WITTIPOL.   In your hearing: so
  You interrupt us not.

FITZDOTTREL.   For the short space
  You do demand, the fourth part of an hour,
  I think I shall, with some convenient study
  And this good help to boot, bring myself to't.   80

  He shrugs himself up in the cloak.

WITTIPOL. I ask no more.

FITZDOTTREL. Please you, walk to'ard my house.
  Speak what you list; that time is yours; my right
  I have departed with. But not beyond
  A minute, or a second, look for. Length,
  And drawing out, may'advance much to these matches.   85
  And I except all kissing. Kisses are
  Silent petitions still with willing lovers.

WITTIPOL. Lovers? How falls that o' your fancy?

FITZDOTTREL.   Sir,
  I do know somewhat; I forbid all lip-work.

WITTIPOL. I am not eager at forbidden dainties.   90
  Who covets unfit things, denies himself.

FITZDOTTREL. You say well, sir; 'twas prettily said, that same,
  He does, indeed. I'll have no touches, therefore,
  Nor takings by the arms, nor tender circles
  Cast 'bout the waist, but all be done at distance.   95
  Love is brought up with those soft migniard handlings;
  His pulse lies in his palm: and I defend
  All melting joints, and fingers – that's my bargain –
  I do defend 'em, anything like action.

But talk, sir, what you will. Use all the tropes   100
And schemes that Prince Quintilian can afford you:
And much good do your rhetoric's heart. You are welcome, sir.
Engine, God be' wi' you.

WITTIPOL.   Sir, I must condition
To have this gentleman by, a witness.

FITZDOTTREL.   Well,
I am content, so he be silent.

MANLY.   Yes, sir.   105

[MANLY, WITTIPOL and ENGINE *enter the house.*]

FITZDOTTREL. Come Devil, I'll make you room straight. But I'll
show you
First to your mistress, who's no common one,
You must conceive, that brings this gain to see her.
I hope thou'st brought me good luck.

PUG.   I shall do't, sir.

[*Exit with* FITZDOTTREL.]

Act I, Scene v

[FITZDOTTREL'*s House.*]

[*Enter*] WITTIPOL, MANLY [*and* ENGINE].

[WITTIPOL.] Engine, you hope o' your half piece? 'Tis there, sir.
Be gone.

[*Exit* ENGINE.] WITTIPOL *knocks his friend o'the breast.*

Friend Manly, who's within here? Fixed?

MANLY. I am directly in a fit of wonder
What'll be the issue of this conference!

WITTIPOL. For that, ne'er vex yourself till the event.   5
  How like you him?

MANLY.   I would fain see more of him.

WITTIPOL. What think you of this?

MANLY.   I am past degrees of thinking.
  Old Afric, and the new America
  With all their fruit of monsters cannot show
  So just a prodigy.

WITTIPOL.   Could you have believed   10
  Without your sight, a mind so sordid inward,
  Should be so specious, and laid forth abroad,
  To all the show that ever shop, or ware was?

MANLY. I believe anything now, though I confess
  His vices are the most extremities   15
  I ever knew in nature. But, why loves he
  The Devil so?

WITTIPOL.   O sir! For hidden treasure
  He hopes to find: and has proposed himself
  So infinite a mass, as to recover
  He cares not what he parts with, of the present   20
  To his men of art, who are the race may coin him.
  Promise gold-mountains, and the covetous
  Are still most prodigal.

MANLY.   But ha' you faith
  That he will hold his bargain?

WITTIPOL.   O dear sir!
  He will not off on't. Fear him not. I know him.   25
  One baseness still accompanies another.
  See! He is here already, and his wife too.

MANLY. A wondrous handsome creature, as I live!

Act I, Scene vi

[*Enter*] FITZDOTTREL, [*and*] MISTRESS FITZDOTTREL.

[FITZDOTTREL.] Come, wife, this is the gentleman. Nay, blush not.

FRANCES. Why, what do you mean, sir? Ha' you your reason?

FITZDOTTREL.   Wife,
  I do not know that I have lent it forth
  To any one; at least, without a pawn, wife:
  Or that I've eat or drunk the thing of late   5
  That should corrupt it. Wherefore, gentle wife
  Obey, it is thy virtue: hold no acts
  Of disputation.

FRANCES.   Are you not enough
  The talk of feasts and meetings, but you'll still
  Make argument for fresh?

FITZDOTTREL.   Why, careful wedlock,   10
  If I have a longing to have one tale more
  Go of me what is that to thee, dear heart?
  Why shouldst thou envy my delight? Or cross it?
  By being solicitous when it not concerns thee?

FRANCES. Yes, I have share in this. The scorn will fall   15
  As bitterly on me, where both are laughed at.

FITZDOTTREL. Laughed at, sweet bird? Is that the scruple?
    Come, come,
  Thou art a niaise.

  (*A Niaise is a young hawk taken crying out of the nest.*)

              Which of your great houses –
  I will not mean at home, here, but abroad –
  Your families in France, wife, send not forth   20
  Something within the seven year may be laughed at?
  I do not say seven months, nor seven weeks,
  Nor seven days, nor hours: but seven year, wife.
  I give 'em time. Once, within seven year,
  I think they may do something may be laughed at,   25

In France, I keep me there, still. Wherefore, wife,
Let them that list laugh still rather than weep
For me. Here is a cloak cost fifty pound, wife,
Which I can sell for thirty, when I ha' seen
All London in't, and London has seen me.   30
Today I go to the Blackfriars Playhouse,
Sit i' the view, salute all my acquaintance,
Rise up between the acts, let fall my cloak,
Publish a handsome man, and a rich suit,
As that's a special end why we go thither,   35
All that pretend to stand for't o' the stage.
The ladies ask who's that, for they do come
To see us, love, as we do to see them.
Now I shall lose all this for the false fear
Of being laughed at? Yes, wusse. Let 'em laugh, wife,   40
Let me have such another cloak tomorrow.
And let 'em laugh again, wife, and again,
And then grow fat with laughing, and then fatter,
All my young gallants, let 'em bring their friends too:
Shall I forbid 'em? No, let heaven forbid 'em: 45
Or wit, if't have any charge on 'em. Come, thy ear, wife,
Is all I'll borrow of thee. Set your watch, sir,
Thou only art to hear, not speak a word, dove,
To aught he says. That I do gi' you in precept
No less than counsel, on your wifehood, wife,   50
Not though he flatter you, or make court, or love –
As you must look for these – or say, he rail;
Whate'er his arts be, wife, I will have thee
Delude 'em with a trick, thy obstinate silence;
I know advantages; and I love to hit   55
These pragmatic young men at their own weapons.
Is your watch ready? Here my sail bears, for you:
Tack toward him, sweet pinnace. Where's your watch?

He disposes his wife to her place, and sets his watch.

WITTIPOL. I'll set it, sir, with yours.

FRANCES.   I must obey.

MANLY. Her modesty seems to suffer with her beauty,   60
    And so, as if his folly were away,
    It were worth pity.

FITZDOTTREL.   Now th'art right, begin, sir.
    But first, let me repeat the contract briefly.

He repeats his contract again.

I am, sir, to enjoy this cloak I stand in
Freely, and as your gift; upon condition   65
You may as freely speak here to my spouse
Your quarter of an hour, always keeping
The measured distance of your yard, or more,
From my said spouse: and in my sight and hearing.
This is your covenant?

WITTIPOL.   Yes, but you'll allow   70
    For this time spent now?

FITZDOTTREL.   Set 'em so much back.

WITTIPOL. I think I shall not need it.

FITZDOTTREL.   Well, begin, sir,
    There is your bound, sir. Not beyond that rush.

WITTIPOL. If you interrupt me, sir, I shall discloak you.

WITTIPOL begins.

The time I have purchased, lady, is but short;   75
And therefore if I employ it thriftily,
I hope I stand the nearer to my pardon.
I am not here to tell you you are fair,
Or lovely, or how well you dress you, lady,
I'll save myself that eloquence of your glass,   80
Which can speak these things better to you than I.
And 'tis a knowledge wherein fools may be
As wise as a court parliament Nor come I,
With any prejudice or doubt, that you
Should, to the notice of your own worth, need   85
Least revelation. She's a simple woman,

Knows not her good – whoever knows her ill –
And at all carats. That you are the wife
To so much blasted flesh as scarce hath soul,
Instead of salt, to keep it sweet, I think   90
Will ask no witnesses to prove. The cold
Sheets that you lie in, with the watching candle,
That sees how dull to any thaw of beauty,
Pieces, and quarters, half, and whole nights, sometimes,
The devil-given elfin squire, your husband,   95
Doth leave you, quitting here his proper circle
For a much worse i'the walks of Lincoln's Inn,
Under the elms, to'expect the fiend in vain, there,
Will confess for you.

FITZDOTTREL.   I did look for this gear.   99

WITTIPOL. And what a daughter of darkness, he does make you,
Locked up from all society or object;
Your eye not let to look upon a face
Under a conjurer's – or some mould for one,
Hollow, and lean like his – but, by great means
As I now make; your own too sensible sufferings,   105
Without the extraordinary aids
Of spells, or spirits, may assure you, lady.
For my part, I protest 'gainst all such practice,
I work by no false arts, medicines, or charms
To be said forward and backward.

FITZDOTTREL.   No I except –   110

WITTIPOL. Sir, I shall ease you.

He offers to discloak him.

FITZDOTTREL.   Mum.

WITTIPOL.   Nor have I ends, lady,
Upon you more than this: to tell you how Love,
Beauty's good angel, he that waits upon her
At all occasions, and no less than Fortune,
Helps th'adventurous, in me makes that proffer   115
Which never fair one was so fond to lose,

Who could but reach a hand forth to her freedom.
On the first sight I loved you: since which time,
Though I have travelled, I have been in travail
More for this second blessing of your eyes   120
Which now I've purchased, than for all aims else.
Think of it, lady, be your mind as active
As is your beauty: view your object well.
Examine both my fashion, and my years.
Things that are like are soon familiar: 125
And Nature joys still in equality.
Let not the sign o'the husband fright you, lady.
But ere your spring be gone, enjoy it. Flowers
Though fair, are oft but of one morning. Think,
All beauty doth not last until the autumn.   130
You grow old while I tell you this. And such
As cannot use the present are not wise.
If Love and Fortune will take care of use,
Why should our will be wanting? This is all.
What do you answer, lady?

She stands mute.

FITZDOTTREL.   Now the sport comes,   135
  Let him still wait, wait, wait: while the watch goes,
  And the time runs. Wife!

WITTIPOL.   How! Not any word?
  Nay then, I taste a trick in't. Worthy lady,
  I cannot be so false to mine own thoughts
  Of your presumed goodness to conceive   140
  This as your rudeness, which I see's imposed.
  Yet since your cautelous gaoler here stands by you,
  And you're denied the liberty o' the house,
  Let me take warrant, lady, from your silence,
  Which ever is interpreted consent,   145
  To make your answer for you: which shall be
  To as good purpose, as I can imagine,
  And what I think you'd speak.

FITZDOTTREL.   No, no, no, no.

WITTIPOL. I shall resume, sir.

MANLY.   Sir, what do you mean?

WITTIPOL. One interruption more, sir, and you go   150
    Into your hose and doublet, nothing saves you.
    And therefore harken.

He sets MASTER MANLY, *his friend, in her place.*

                              This is for your wife.

MANLY. You must play fair, sir.

WITTIPOL.   Stand for me, good friend.

And [WITTIPOL] speaks for her.

Troth, sir, 'tis more then true that you have uttered
Of my unequal, and so sordid match here,   155
With all the circumstances of my bondage.
I have a husband, and a two-legged one,
But such a moonling, as no wit of man
Or roses can redeem from being an ass.
He's grown too much, the story of men's mouths   160
To scape his lading: should I make't my study,
And lay all ways, yea, call mankind to help
To take his burden off, why this one act
Of his, to let his wife out to be courted,
And at a price, proclaims his asinine nature   165
So loud as I am weary of my title to him.
But sir, you seem a gentleman of virtue
No less than blood; and one that every way
Looks as he were of too good quality,
To entrap a credulous woman, or betray her: 170
Since you have paid thus dear, sir, for a visit,
And made such venture on your wit and charge
Merely to see me, or at most to speak to me,
I were too stupid, or – what's worse – ingrate
Not to return your venture. Think but how   175
I may with safety do it; I shall trust
My love and honour to you, and presume,

You'll ever husband both against this husband;
Who, if we chance to change his liberal ears
To other ensigns, and with labour make 180
A new beast of him, as he shall deserve,
Cannot complain he is unkindly dealt with.
This day he is to go to a new play, sir,
From whence no fear, no, nor authority,
Scarcely the King's command, sir, will restrain him, 185
Now you have fitted him with a stage-garment
For the mere name's sake, were there nothing else:
And many more such journeys he will make,
Which, if they now, or any time hereafter,
Offer us opportunity, you hear, sir, 190
Who'll be as glad, and forward to embrace,
Meet, and enjoy it cheerfully as you.

He shifts to his own place again.

I humbly thank you, lady.

FITZDOTTREL.   Keep your ground, sir.

WITTIPOL. Will you be lightened?

FITZDOTTREL.   Mum.

WITTIPOL.   And but I am,
By the sad contract, thus to take my leave of you 195
At this so envious distance, I had taught
Our lips ere this to seal the happy mixture
Made of our souls. But we must both now yield
To the necessity. Do not think yet, lady,
But I can kiss, and touch, and laugh, and whisper, 200
And do those crowning courtships too, for which
Day and the public have allowed no name,
But now my bargain binds me. 'Twere rude injury
To'importune more, or urge a noble nature
To what of its own bounty it is prone to: 205
Else I should speak – But, lady, I love so well,
As I will hope you'll do so too. I have done, sir.

FITZDOTTREL. Well then I ha' won?

WITTIPOL.   Sir. And I may win, too.

FITZDOTTREL. O yes! No doubt on't. I'll take careful order
   That she shall hang forth ensigns at the window   210
   To tell you I am absent. Or I'll keep
   Three or four footmen ready still of purpose
   To run and fetch you, at her longings, sir.
   I'll go bespeak me straight a gilt caroche
   For her and you to take the air in. Yes   215
   Into Hyde Park, and thence into Blackfriars,
   Visit the painters, where you may see pictures,
   And note the properest limbs, and how to make 'em.
   Or what do you say unto a middling gossip?
   To bring you aye together at her lodging?   220
   Under pretext of teaching o'my wife
   Some rare receipt of drawing almond milk? Ha?
   It shall be a part of my care. Good sir, God be'wi' you.
   I ha' kept the contract and the cloak is mine.

WITTIPOL. Why, much good do't you sir; it may fall out   225
   That you ha' bought it dear, though I ha' not sold it.

FITZDOTTREL. A pretty riddle! Fare you well, good sir.

He turns his wife about.

   Wife, your face this way, look on me: and think
   You've had a wicked dream, wife, and forget it.

MANLY. This is the strangest motion I e'er saw.   230

   [*Exeunt* MANLY *and* WITTIPOL.]

FITZDOTTREL. Now wife, sits this fair cloak the worse upon me
   For my great sufferings or your little patience? Ha?
   They laugh, you think?

FRANCES.   Why sir, and you might see't,
   What thought they have of you, may be soon collected
   By the young gentleman's speech.

FITZDOTTREL.   Young gentleman?   235
   Death! You are in love with him, are you? Could he not

Be named the gentleman without the young?
Up to your cabin again.

FRANCES.   My cage, you' were best
To call it.

FITZDOTTREL. Yes, sing there. You'd fain be making
Blanc-manger with him at your mother's. I know you.   240
Go, get you up.

[*Exit* MISTRESS FITZDOTTREL.]

[*Enter* PUG.]

                How now! What say you, Devil?

Act I, Scene vii

[PUG.] Here is one Engine, sir, desires to speak with you.

FITZDOTTREL. I thought he brought some news of a broker! Well,
Let him come in, good Devil; fetch him else.

[*Exit* PUG.]

[*Enter* ENGINE.]

O, my fine Engine! What's th'affair? More cheats?

ENGINE. No sir, the wit, the brain, the great projector,   5
I told you of, is newly come to town.

FITZDOTTREL. Where, Engine?

ENGINE.   I ha' brought him – he's without –
Ere he pulled off his boots, sir, but so followed
For businesses.

FITZDOTTREL. But what is a projector?
I would conceive.

ENGINE.   Why one, sir, that projects   10

Ways to enrich men, or to make 'em great,
By suits, by marriages, by undertakings
According as he sees they humour it.

FITZDOTTREL. Can he not conjure at all?

ENGINE.   I think he can, sir –
 To tell you true – but you do know, of late   15
 The State hath ta'en such note of 'em, and compelled 'em
 To enter such great bonds, they dare not practise.

FITZDOTTREL. 'Tis true, and I lie fallow for't the while!

ENGINE. O sir! You'll grow the richer for the rest.

FITZDOTTREL. I hope I shall: but Engine, you do talk   20
 Somewhat too much o'my courses. My cloak-customer
 Could tell me strange particulars.

ENGINE.   By my means?

FITZDOTTREL. How should he have 'em else?

ENGINE.   You do not know, sir,
 What he has: and by what arts! A moneyed man, sir,
 And is as great with your almanack-men, as you are!   25

FITZDOTTREL. That gallant?

ENGINE.   You make the other wait too long, here:
 And he is extreme punctual.

FITZDOTTREL.   Is he a gallant?

ENGINE. Sir, you shall see: he's in his riding suit,
 As he comes now from Court. But hear him speak:
 Minister matter to him, and then tell me.   30

Act II, Scene i

[*Enter*] MERECRAFT, TRAINS [*and three* WAITERS].

MERECRAFT. Sir, money's a whore, a bawd, a drudge,
    Fit to run out on errands: let her go.
    Via pecunia! When she's run and gone,
    And fled and dead, then will I fetch her again
    With aqua-vitae out of an old hogshead!   5
    While there are lees of wine, or dregs of beer,
    I'll never want her! Coin her out of cobwebs,
    Dust, but I'll have her! Raise wool upon eggshells,
    Sir, and make grass grow out o' marrow-bones,
    To make her come.

To a WAITER.

                  Commend me to your mistress,   10
    Say, let the thousand pound but be had ready
    And it is done.

[*Exit* FIRST WAITER.]

            I would but see the creature
    Of flesh and blood, the man, the prince, indeed,
    That could employ so many millions
    As I would help him to.

FITZDOTTREL.   How talks he? Millions?   15

MERECRAFT. I'll give you an account of this tomorrow.

To another.

Yes I will talk no less and do it too –

[*Exit* SECOND WAITER.]

If they were myriads – and without the devil

By direct means: it shall be good in law.

ENGINE.   Sir.

To a third.

MERECRAFT. Tell Master Woodcock, I'll not fail to meet him   20
  Upon th' Exchange at night. Pray him to have
  The writings there and we'll dispatch it.

  [*Exit* THIRD WAITER.] *He turns to* FITZDOTTREL.

                                                      Sir,

You are a gentleman of a good presence,
A handsome man. I have considered you
As a fit stock to graft honours upon.   25
I have a project to make you a duke, now.
That you must be one, within so many months
As I set down out of true reason of state,
You sha' not avoid it. But you must harken, then.

ENGINE. Harken? Why sir, do you doubt his ears? Alas!   30
  You do not know Master Fitzdottrel.

FITZDOTTREL. He does not know me indeed. I thank you,
    Engine,
  For rectifying him.

MERECRAFT.   Good!

He turns to ENGINE.

                          Why, Engine, then
I'll tell you. I see you ha' credit here,
And that you can keep counsel, I'll not question.   35
He shall but be an undertaker with me
In a most feasible business. It shall cost him
Nothing.

ENGINE.   Good, sir.

MERECRAFT.   Except he please, but's count'nance –
  That I will have – to'appear in't to great men,
  For which I'll make him one. He shall not draw   40

A string of's purse. I'll drive his patent for him.
We'll take in citizens, commoners, and aldermen,
To bear the charge, and blow 'em off again
Like so many dead flies, when 'tis carried.
The thing is for recovery of drowned land,   45
Whereof the Crown's to have his moiety
If it be owner; else, the Crown and owners
To share that moiety, and the recoverers
To'enjoy the tother moiety for their charge.

ENGINE. Throughout England?

MERECRAFT.   Yes, which will arise   50
To eighteen millions, seven the first year:
I have computed all and made my survey
Unto an acre. I'll begin at the pan,
Not at the skirts as some ha' done, and lost
All that they wrought, their timber-work, their trench,   55
Their banks all borne away, or else filled up
By the next winter. Tut, they never went
The way: I'll have it all.

ENGINE.   A gallant tract
Of land it is!

MERECRAFT. 'Twill yield a pound an acre.
We must let cheap, ever, at first. But sir,   60
This looks too large for you, I see. Come hither,
We'll have a less. Here's a plain fellow, you see him,

[*He points to* TRAINS.]

Has his black bag of papers there, in buckram,
Wi' not be sold for th'earldom of Pancridge: draw,
Gi' me out one, by chance.

[TRAINS *pulls out a paper from the bag.*]

                    Project 4. Dog-skins!   65
Twelve thousand pound! The very worst, at first.

FITZDOTTREL. Pray you, let's see't, sir.

MERECRAFT.   'Tis a toy, a trifle!

FITZDOTTREL. Trifle! Twelve thousand pound for dog-skins?

MERECRAFT.   Yes,
 But by my way of dressing, you must know, sir,
 And med'cining the leather to a height   70
 Of improved ware, like your borachio
 Of Spain, sir, I can fetch nine thousand for't –

ENGINE. Of the King's glover?

MERECRAFT.   Yes, how heard you that?

ENGINE. Sir, I do know you can.

MERECRAFT.   Within this hour:
 And reserve half my secret. Pluck another;   75
 See if thou hast a happier hand:

He plucks out the second [paper]. Bottle-ale.
      I thought so.
 The very next worse to it! Bottle-ale.
 Yet, this is two and twenty thousand! Prithee
 Pull out another, two or three.

FITZDOTTREL.   Good. Stay, friend,
 By bottle-ale, two and twenty thousand pound?   80

MERECRAFT. Yes, sir, it's cast to penny-halfpenny-farthing
 O' the backside, there you may see it, read:
 I will not bate a harrington o' the sum.
 I'll win it i'my water, and my malt,
 My furnaces, and hanging o'my coppers,   85
 The tunning, and the subtlety o' my yeast;
 And then the earth of my bottles, which I dig,
 Turn up, and steep, and work, and neal myself
 To a degree of porcelain. You will wonder
 At my proportions, what I will put up   90
 In seven years! For so long time I ask
 For my invention. I will save in cork,
 In my mere stoppling, 'bove three thousand pound

Within that term: by gouging of 'em out
Just to the size of my bottles, and not slicing.   95
There's infinite loss i' that. What hast thou there?

He draws out another, Raisins.

O' making wine of raisins: this is in hand, now.

ENGINE. Is not that strange, sir, to make wine of raisins?

MERECRAFT. Yes, and as true a wine, as th'wines of France,
Or Spain, or Italy. Look of what grape   100
My raisin is, that wine I'll render perfect,
As of the muscatel grape, I'll render muscatel;
Of the canary, his; the claret, his;
So of all kinds: and bate you of the prices
Of wine throughout the kingdom, half in half.   105

ENGINE. But how, sir, if you raise the other commodity,
Raisins?

MERECRAFT. Why, then I'll make it out of blackberries:
And it shall do the same. 'Tis but more art,
And the charge less. Take out another.

FITZDOTTREL.   No, good sir.
Save you the trouble, I'll not look nor hear   110
Of any but your first, there; the drowned land:
If 't will do as you say.

MERECRAFT.   Sir, there's not place
To gi' you demonstration of these things.
They are a little too subtle. But I could show you
Such a necessity in't, as you must be   115
But what you please, against the received heresy
That England bears no dukes. Keep you the land, sir,
The greatness of th'estate shall throw't upon you.
If you like better turning it to money,
What may not you, sir, purchase with that wealth?   120
Say you should part with two o' your millions
To be the thing you would, who would not do't?
As I protest I will, out of my dividend,

Lay for some pretty principality
In Italy, from the Church. Now you perhaps   125
Fancy the smoke of England rather? But –
Ha' you no private room, sir, to draw to,
T' enlarge ourselves more upon?

FITZDOTTREL.   O yes, Devil!

MERECRAFT. These, sir, are businesses ask to be carried
With caution, and in cloud.

FITZDOTTREL.   I apprehend   130
They do so, sir.

[*Enter* PUG.]

                Devil, which way is your mistress?

PUG. Above, sir, in her chamber.

FITZDOTTREL.   O that's well.
Then this way, good sir.

MERECRAFT.   I shall follow you. Trains,
Gi' me the bag, and go you presently
Commend my service to my Lady Tailbush.   135
Tell her I am come from Court this morning; say,
I've got our business moved, and well: entreat her
That she give you the fourscore angels, and see 'em
Disposed of to my counsel, Sir Paul Eitherside.
Sometime today I'll wait upon her Ladyship   140
With the relation.

[*Exit* TRAINS.]

ENGINE.   Sir, of what dispatch
He is! Do you mark?

MERECRAFT. Engine, when did you see
My cousin Everill? Keeps he still your quarter?
I' the Bermudas?

ENGINE.   Yes, sir, he was writing
This morning very hard.

MERECRAFT.   Be not you known to him,   145
   That I am come to town: I have effected
   A business for him, but I would have it take him
   Before he thinks for't.

ENGINE.   Is it past?

MERECRAFT.   Not yet.
   'Tis well o' the way.

ENGINE.   O sir! Your worship takes
   Infinite pains.

MERECRAFT.   I love friends to be active: 150
   A sluggish nature puts off man and kind.

ENGINE. And such a blessing follows it.

MERECRAFT.   I thank
   My fate. Pray you, let's be private, sir?

FITZDOTTREL.   In here.

MERECRAFT. Where none may interrupt us.

   [*Exit, with* ENGINE.]

FITZDOTTREL.   You hear, Devil,
   Lock the street doors fast and let no one in –   155
   Except they be this gentleman's followers –
   To trouble me. Do you mark? You've heard and seen
   Something today; and by it you may gather
   Your mistress is a fruit that's worth the stealing,
   And therefore worth the watching. Be you sure now   160
   You've all your eyes about you; and let in
   No lace-woman, nor bawd that brings French masks
   And cut-works. See you? Nor old crones with wafers
   To convey letters. Nor no youths, disguised
   Like country wives, with cream, and marrow-puddings.   165
   Much knavery may be vented in a pudding,
   Much bawdy intelligence: they're shrewd ciphers.
   Nor turn the key to any neighbour's need –
   Be't but to kindle fire, or beg a little;

Put it out, rather, all out, to an ash,   170
That they may see no smoke. Or water, spill it:
Knock o' the empty tubs that by the sound
They may be forbid entry. Say we are robbed
If any come to borrow a spoon, or so.
I wi' not have good fortune, or God's blessing   175
Let in while I am busy.

PUG.   I'll take care sir:
They sha' not trouble you, if they would.

FITZDOTTREL.   Well, do so.

　　　[*Exit* FITZDOTTREL.]

Act II, Scene ii

PUG. I have no singular service of this now!
　　　Nor no superlative master! I shall wish
　　　To be in Hell again at leisure! Bring
　　　A Vice from thence! That had been such a subtlety
　　　As to bring broad-clothes hither, or transport   5
　　　Fresh oranges into Spain. I find it now;
　　　My chief was i' the right. Can any fiend
　　　Boast of a better Vice than here by nature
　　　And art they're owners of? Hell ne'er own me
　　　But I am taken! The fine tract of it   10
　　　Pulls me along! To hear men such professors
　　　Grown in our subtlest sciences! My first act now
　　　Shall be to make this master of mine cuckold:
　　　The primitive work of darkness I will practise!
　　　I will deserve so well of my fair mistress,   15
　　　By my discoveries first, my counsels after,
　　　And keeping counsel after that, as who
　　　So ever is one, I'll be another; sure
　　　I'll ha' my share. Most delicate damned flesh

She will be! O that I could stay time now,   20
Midnight will come too fast upon me, I fear,
To cut my pleasure –

[*Enter* MISTRESS FITZDOTTREL.]

FRANCES.   Look at the back door;
One knocks, see who it is.

She sends DEVIL *out.*

PUG [*aside*].   Dainty she-devil!

   [*Exit.*]

FRANCES. I cannot get this venture of the cloak
Out of my fancy; nor the gentleman's way   25
He took, which though 'twere strange, yet 'twas handsome
And had a grace withal beyond the newness.
Sure he will think me that dull stupid creature
He said, and may conclude it, if I find out
Some thought to thank th' attempt. He did presume,   30
By all the carriage of it on my brain,
For answer; and will swear 'tis very barren,
If it can yield him no return.

   DEVIL *returns.*

                             Who is it?

PUG. Mistress, it is – but first, let me assure
The excellence of mistresses, I am,   35
Although my master's man, my mistress' slave,
The servant of her secrets and sweet turns,
And know what fitly will conduce to either.

FRANCES. What's this? I pray you come to yourself and think
What your part is: to make an answer. Tell   40
Who is it at the door?

PUG.   The gentleman, mistress,
Who was at the cloak-charge to speak with you
This morning, who expects only to take
Some small commandments from you, what you please,

Worthy your form, he says, and gentlest manners.   45

FRANCES. O! You'll anon prove his hired man, I fear;
    What has he given you for this message? Sir,
    Bid him put off his hopes of straw, and leave
    To spread his nets in view, thus. Though they take
    Master Fitzdottrel, I am no such fowl –   50
    Nor fair one, tell him, will be had with stalking.
    And wish him to forbear his acting to me
    At the gentleman's chamber-window in Lincoln's Inn there,
    That opens to my gallery: else, I swear,
    T' acquaint my husband with his folly, and leave him   55
    To the just rage of his offended jealousy.
    Or if your master's sense be not so quick
    To right me, tell him I shall find a friend
    That will repair me. Say I will be quiet
    In mine own house! Pray you, in those words give it him.   60

PUG. This is some fool turned.

He goes out.

FRANCES.   If he be the master
    Now of that state and wit which I allow him,
    Sure he will understand me: I durst not
    Be more direct. For this officious fellow,
    My husband's new groom, is a spy upon me   65
    I find already. Yet if he but tell him
    This in my words, he cannot but conceive
    Himself both apprehended and requited.
    I would not have him think he met a statue
    Or spoke to one not there, though I were silent.   70

    [*Re-enter* PUG.]

    How now? Ha'you told him?

PUG.   Yes.

FRANCES.   And what says he?

PUG. Says he? That which myself would say to you, if I durst.
    That you are proud, sweet mistress! And withal

A little ignorant to entertain
The good that's proffered; and, by your beauty's leave,   75
Not all so wise as some true politic wife
Would be: who having matched with such a nupson –
I speak it with my master's peace – whose face
Hath left t'accuse him now, for't doth confess him,
What you can make him; will yet, out of scruple   80
And a spiced conscience, defraud the poor gentleman,
At least delay him in the thing he longs for,
And makes it his whole study, how to compass
Only a title. Could but he write cuckold,
He had his ends. For, look you –

FRANCES.   This can be   85
     None but my husband's wit.

PUG.   My precious mistress!

FRANCES. It creaks his engine: the groom never durst
     Be, else, so saucy. –

PUG.   If it were not clearly
     His worshipful ambition, and the top of it,
     The very forked top too, why should he   90
     Keep you thus mured up in a back room, mistress,
     Allow you ne'er a casement to the street,
     Fear of engendering by the eyes with gallants,
     Forbid you paper, pen and ink, like ratsbane,
     Search your half pint of muscatel lest a letter   95
     Be sunk i' the pot, and hold your new-laid egg
     Against the fire, lest any charm be writ there?
     Will you make benefit of truth, dear mistress,
     If I do tell it you: I do't not often?
     I am set over you, employed, indeed,   100
     To watch your steps, your looks, your very breathings,
     And to report them to him. Now if you
     Will be a true, right, delicate sweet mistress,
     Why we will make a Cokes of this wise master:
     We will, my mistress, an absolute fine Cokes,   105
     And mock to air all the deep diligences

Of such a solemn, and effectual ass,
An ass to so good purpose as we'll use him.
I will contrive it so that you shall go
To plays, to masques, to meetings, and to feasts.   110
For, why is all this rigging and fine tackle, mistress,
If you neat handsome vessels of good sail,
Put not forth ever and anon with your nets
Abroad into the world? It is your fishing.
There you shall choose your friends, your servants, lady,   115
Your squires of honour; I'll convey your letters,
Fetch answers, do you all the offices
That can belong to your blood and beauty. And,
For the variety, at my times, although
I am not in due symmetry the man   120
Of that proportion, or in rule
Of physic of the just complexion,
Or of that truth of picardill in clothes
To boast a sovereignty o'er ladies, yet
I know to do my turns, sweet mistress. Come, kiss –   125

FRANCES. How now!

PUG.   Dear delicate mistress, I am your slave,
Your little worm that loves you, your fine monkey;
Your dog, your jack, your Pug, that longs to be
Styled o' your pleasures.

She thinks her husband watches.

FRANCES.   Hear you all this, sir? Pray you,
Come from your standing, do! A little spare   130
Yourself, sir, from your watch, to'applaud your squire,
That so well follows your instructions!

Act II, Scene iii

[*Enter*] FITZDOTTREL.

FITZDOTTREL. How now, sweetheart? What's the matter?

FRANCES.   Good!
    You are a stranger to the plot! You set not
    Your saucy Devil here to tempt your wife
    With all the insolent uncivil language,
    Or action, he could vent?

FITZDOTTREL.   Did you so, Devil?   5

FRANCES. Not you? You were not planted i'your hole to hear him
    Upo' the stairs? Or here, behind the hangings?
    I do not know your qualities? He durst do it,
    And you not give directions?

FITZDOTTREL.   You shall see, wife,
    Whether he durst, or no: and what it was   10
    I did direct.

PUG.   Sweet mistress, are you mad?

Her HUSBAND *goes out, and enters presently with a cudgel upon him*
[*and beats* PUG].

FITZDOTTREL. You most mere rogue! You open manifest villain!
    You fiend apparent, you! You declared hellhound!

PUG. Good sir!

FITZDOTTREL. Good knave, good rascal, and good traitor!
    Now I do find you parcel-Devil, indeed.   15
    Upon'the point of trust? I'your first charge?
    The very day o'your probation?
    To tempt your mistress? You do see, good wedlock,
    How I directed him.

FRANCES.   Why where, sir, were you?

After a pause.

FITZDOTTREL. Nay, there is one blow more for exercise   20
    I told you, I should do it.

PUG.   Would you had done, sir.

FITZDOTTREL. Oh wife, the rarest man! Yet there's another
    To put you in mind o'the last.

He strikes him again.

                Such a brave man, wife,
    Within, he has his projects, and does vent 'em,
    The gallantest! Were you tentiginous? Ha?   25

And again.

    Would you be acting of the incubus?
    Did her silks' rustling move you?

PUG.   Gentle sir!

FITZDOTTREL. Out of my sight. If thy name were not Devil,
    Thou shouldst not stay a minute with me. In,
    Go, yet stay, yet go too. I am resolved   30
    What I will do: and you shall know't aforehand.
    Soon as the gentleman is gone, do you hear?
    I'll help your lisping.

    DEVIL *goes out.*

              Wife, such a man, wife!
    He has such plots! He will make me a duke!
    No less, by heaven! Six mares to your coach, wife!   35
    That's your proportion! And your coachman bald!
    Because he shall be bare, enough. Do not you laugh,
    We are looking for a place and all i' the map
    What to be of. Have faith, be not an infidel.
    You know I am not easy to be gulled.   40
    I swear when I have my millions, else, I'll make
    Another duchess, if you ha' not faith.

FRANCES. You'll ha' too much, I fear, in these false spirits.

FITZDOTTREL. Spirits? O, no such thing! Wife! Wit, mere wit!
    This man defies the Devil, and all his works!   45
    He does't by engine and devices, he!
    He has his winged ploughs that go with sails,

Will plough you forty acres at once! And mills
Will spout you water, ten miles off! All Crowland
Is ours, wife; and the fens, from us in Norfolk   50
To the utmost bound of Lincolnshire! We have viewed it,
And measured it within all, by the scale!
The richest tract of land, love, i'the kingdom!
There will be made seventeen, or eighteen millions;
Or more, as 't may be handled! Wherefore think,   55
Sweetheart, if thou'hast a fancy to one place
More than another, to be Duchess of,
Now, name it: I will ha't what e'er it cost,
If 'twill be had for money, either here,
Or'in France, or Italy.

FRANCES.   You ha' strange fantasies!   60

Act II, Scene iv

[*Enter*] MERECRAFT [*and*] ENGINE.

MERECRAFT. Where are you, sir?

FITZDOTTREL.   I see thou hast no talent
    This way, wife. Up to thy gallery; do, chuck,
    Leave us to talk of it who understand it.

    [*Exit* MISTRESS FITZDOTTREL.]

MERECRAFT. I think we ha' found a place to fit you now, sir.
    Gloucester.

FITZDOTTREL. O no, I'll none!

MERECRAFT.   Why, sir?

FITZDOTTREL.   'Tis fatal.   5

MERECRAFT. That you say right in. Spenser, I think, the younger,
    Had his last honour thence. But he was but Earl.

FITZDOTTREL. I know not that, sir. But Thomas of Woodstock,
     I'm sure, was Duke, and he was made away
     At Calais; as Duke Humphrey was at Bury;   10
     And Richard the third, you know what end he came to.

MERECRAFT. By my'faith you are cunning i'the-chronicle, sir.

FITZDOTTREL. No, I confess I ha't from the play-books,
     And think they're more authentic.

ENGINE.   That's sure, sir.

MERECRAFT. What say you to this then?

He whispers him of a place.

FITZDOTTREL.   No, a noble house   15
     Pretends to that. I will do no man wrong.

MERECRAFT. Then take one proposition more, and hear it
     As past exception.

FITZDOTTREL.   What's that?

MERECRAFT.   To be
     Duke of those lands you shall recover: take
     Your title thence, sir, Duke of the Drowned-lands,   20
     Or Drowned-land.

FITZDOTTREL.   Ha! That last has a good sound!
     I like it well. The Duke of Drowned-land?

ENGINE.   Yes;
     It goes like Greenland, sir, if you mark it.

MERECRAFT.   Ay,
     And drawing thus your honour from the work,
     You make the reputation of that greater,   25
     And stay 't the longer i' your name.

FITZDOTTREL.   'Tis true.
     Drowned-lands will live in Drowned-land!

MERECRAFT.   Yes, when you
     Ha' no foot left, as that must be, sir, one day.
     And, though it tarry in your heirs some forty,

Fifty descents, the longer liver at last, yet,   30
Must thrust 'em out on't: if no quirk in law,
Or odd vice o'their own not do't first.
We see those changes daily: the fair lands,
That were the client's, are the lawyer's now;
And those rich manors there of good man tailor's   35
Had once more wood upon 'em than the yard
By which they'were measured out for the last purchase.
Nature hath these vicissitudes. She makes
No man a state of perpetuity, sir.

FITZDOTTREL. You're i' the right. Let's in then, and conclude. 40

He spies DEVIL.

I' my sight again? I'll talk with you anon.

[*Exeunt* FITZDOTTREL, MERECRAFT *and* ENGINE.]

Act II, Scene v

[*Enter* PUG.]

PUG. Sure he will geld me if I stay; or worse,
Pluck out my tongue – one o'the two. This fool,
There is no trusting of him: and to quit him
Were a contempt against my chief, past pardon.
It was a shrewd disheartening this, at first!   5
Who would ha' thought a woman so well harnessed,
Or rather well caparisoned, indeed,
That wears such petticoats and lace to her smocks,
Broad seaming laces as I see 'em hang there,
And garters, which are lost, if she can show 'em,   10
Could ha' done this? Hell! Why is she so brave?
It cannot be to please Duke Dottrel, sure,
Nor the dull pictures in her gallery,
Nor her own dear reflection in her glass.

Yet that may be: I have known many of 'em   15
Begin their pleasure, but none end it, there.
That I consider, as I go along with it.
They may for want of better company,
Or that they think the better, spend an hour,
Two, three, or four, discoursing with their shadow;   20
But sure they have a farther speculation.
No woman dressed with so much care and study,
Doth dress herself in vain. I'll vex this problem
A little more, before I leave it, sure.

[*Exit.*]

Act II, Scene vi

[*Enter*] WITTIPOL [*and*] MANLY [*at a window opposite* MISTRESS
FITZDOTTREL's *gallery.*]

WITTIPOL. This was a fortune, happy above thought,
    That this should prove thy chamber, which I feared
    Would be my greatest trouble! This must be
    The very window and that the room.

MANLY.   It is.
    I now remember I have often seen there   5
    A woman, but I never marked her much.

WITTIPOL. Where was your soul, friend?

MANLY.   Faith, but now and then
    Awake unto those objects.

WITTIPOL.   You pretend so.
    Let me not live if I am not in love
    More with her wit for this direction now,   10
    Than with her form, though I ha' praised that prettily
    Since I saw her and you today. Read those.

He gives him a paper, wherein is the copy of a song.

They'll go unto the air you love so well.
Try 'em unto the note. May be the music
Will call her sooner.

[*Enter* MISTRESS FITZDOTTREL *in her gallery.*]

'Slight, she's here. Sing quickly.   15

FRANCES. Either he understood him not, or else
The fellow was not faithful in delivery
Of what I bade. And I am justly paid,
That might have made my profit of his service,
But by mistaking have drawn on his envy,   20
And done the worse defeat upon myself.

MANLY *sings.* PUG *enters,* [*and*] *perceives it.*

How! Music? Then he may be there: and is, sure.

PUG [*aside*]. O! Is it so? Is there the interview?
Have I drawn to you at last, my cunning lady?
The devil is an ass! Fooled off! And beaten!   25
Nay, made an instrument! And could not scent it!
Well, since you've shown the malice of a woman
No less than her true wit and learning, mistress,
I'll try if little Pug have the malignity
To recompense it, and so save his danger.   30
'Tis not the pain, but the discredit of it;
The Devil should not keep a body entire.

[*Exit.*]

WITTIPOL. Away, fall back, she comes.

MANLY.   I'll leave you, sir,
The master of my chamber. I have business.   34

[*Exit.*]

WITTIPOL. Mistress!

FRANCES.   You make me paint, sir.

WITTIPOL.   They're fair colours,

Lady, and natural! I did receive
Some commands from you lately, gentle lady,
But so perplexed and wrapped in the delivery,
As I may fear t'have misinterpreted: 40
But must make suit still to be near your grace.

This scene is acted at two windows, as out of two contiguous buildings.

FRANCES. Who is there with you, sir?

WITTIPOL.   None, but myself.
It falls out, lady, to be a dear friend's lodging.
Wherein there's some conspiracy of fortune
With your poor servant's blessed affections.

FRANCES. Who was it sung?

WITTIPOL.   He, lady, but he's gone   45
Upon my entreaty of him, seeing you
Approach the window. Neither need you doubt him,
If he were here. He is too much a gentleman.

FRANCES. Sir, if you judge me by this simple action,
And by the outward habit, and complexion   50
Of easiness it hath to your design,
You may with justice say I am a woman,
And a strange woman. But when you shall please
To bring but that concurrence of my fortune
To memory, which today yourself did urge,   55
It may beget some favour like excuse,
Though none like reason.

WITTIPOL.   No, my tuneful mistress?
Then surely Love hath none; nor Beauty any;
Nor Nature violenced, in both these:
With all whose gentle tongues you speak at once.   60
I thought I had enough removed already
That scruple from your breast, and left you'all reason,
When, through my morning's perspective, I showed you
A man so above excuse, as he is the cause
Why anything is to be done upon him: 65
And nothing called an injury, misplaced.

I rather now had hope to show you how Love,
By his accesses, grows more natural:
And what was done this morning with such force
Was but devised to serve the present, then.   70

*He grows more familiar in his courtship, plays with her paps, kisseth
her hands, etc.*

That since Love hath the honour to approach
These sister-swelling breasts, and touch this soft,
And rosy hand, he hath the skill to draw
Their nectar forth, with kissing; and could make
More wanton salts from this brave promontory   75
Down to this valley, than the nimble roe;
Could play the hopping sparrow, 'bout these nets,
And sporting squirrel in these crisped groves;
Bury himself in every silkworm's kell
Is here unravelled; run into the snare,   80
Which every hair is, cast into a curl
To catch a Cupid flying; bathe himself
In milk and roses here, and dry him there;
Warm his cold hands to play with this smooth, round,
And well-turned chin, as with the billiard ball;   85
Roll on these lips, the banks of love, and there
At once both plant and gather kisses. Lady,
Shall I, with what I have made today here, call
All sense to wonder, and all faith to sign
The mysteries revealed in your form?   90
And will Love pardon me the blasphemy
I uttered, when I said a glass could speak
Thus beauty, or that fools had power to judge it?

[*Sings.*]

Do but look on her eyes! They do light –
    All that Love's world compriseth!   95
Do but look on her hair! It is bright
    As Love's star, when it riseth!
Do but mark, her forehead's smoother,
    Than words that soothe her!

And from her arched brows, such a grace   100
  Sheds itself through the face,
As alone, there triumphs to the life
  All the gain, all the good, of the elements' strife!

Have you seen but a bright lily grow,
  Before rude hands have touched it?   105
Have you marked but the fall of the snow,
  Before the soil hath smutched it?
Have you felt the wool o'the beaver?
  Or swansdown, ever?
Or have smelt o'the bud o'the briar?   110
  Or the nard i' the fire?
Or have tasted the bag o'the bee?
  O, so white! O, so soft! O, so sweet is she!

Act II, Scene vii

Her husband appears at her back.

FITZDOTTREL. Is she so, sir? And I will keep her so
  If I know how, or can: that wit of man
  Will do't, I'll go no farther. At this window
  She shall no more be buzzed at. Take your leave on't.
  If you be sweetmeats, wedlock, or sweet flesh,   5
  All's one: I do not love this hum about you.
  A fly-blown wife is not so proper. In:

He speaks out of his wife's window.

For you, sir, look to hear from me.

WITTIPOL.   So I do, sir.

FITZDOTTREL. No, but in other terms. There's no man offers
  This to my wife, but pays for't.

WITTIPOL.   That have I, sir.   10

FITZDOTTREL. Nay, then, I tell you, you are –

WITTIPOL.   What am I, sir?

FITZDOTTREL. Why, that I'll think on, when I ha' cut your throat.

WITTIPOL. Go, you are an ass.

FITZDOTTREL.   I am resolved on't, sir.

WITTIPOL. I think you are.

FITZDOTTREL.   To call you to a reckoning.

WITTIPOL. Away, you broker's block, you property!   15

FITZDOTTREL. 'Slight, if you strike me, I'll strike your mistress.

He strikes his wife.

WITTIPOL. O! I could shoot mine eyes at him for that, now;
    Or leave my teeth in'him, were they cuckold's bane
    Enough to kill him. What prodigious,
    Blind, and most wicked change of fortune's this?   20
    I ha' no air of patience: all my veins
    Swell, and my sinews start at iniquity of it.
    I shall break, break.

    [Exit.] The DEVIL *speaks below.*

PUG.   This, for the malice of it,
    And my revenge may pass! But now my conscience
    Tells me I have profited the cause of Hell   25
    But little, in the breaking-off their loves.
    Which, if some other act of mine repair not,
    I shall hear ill of in my account.

    FITZDOTTREL *enters with his wife as come down.*

FITZDOTTREL.   O, bird!
    Could you do this? 'Gainst me? And at this time, now?
    When I was so employed wholly for you,   30
    Drowned i'my care – more than the land I swear,
    I've hope to win – to make you peerless? Studying

For footmen for you, fine-paced ushers, pages,
To serve you o'the knee; with what knight's wife
To bear your train, and sit with your four women   35
In council, and receive intelligences
From foreign parts; to dress you at all pieces!
You've almost turned my good affection to you;
Soured my sweet thoughts, all my pure purposes;
I could now find i'my very heart to make   40
Another lady Duchess and depose you.
Well, go your ways in.

[*Exit* MISTRESS FITZDOTTREL.]

                        Devil, you have redeemed all.
I do forgive you. And I'll do you good.

[*Exit* PUG.]

Act II, Scene viii

[*Enter*] MERECRAFT [*and*] ENGINE.

[MERECRAFT.] Why ha' you these excursions? Where ha' you
    been, sir?

FITZDOTTREL. Where I ha' been vexed a little, with a toy!

MERECRAFT. O, sir! No toys must trouble your grave head,
    Now it is growing to be great. You must
    Be above all those things.

FITZDOTTREL.   Nay, nay, so I will.   5

MERECRAFT. Now you are to'ard the lord, you must put off
    The man, sir.

ENGINE.   He says true.

MERECRAFT.   You must do nothing

As you ha' done it heretofore; not know,
Or salute any man.

ENGINE.   That was your bedfellow
    The other month.

MERECRAFT.   The other month? The week.   10
    Thou dost not know the privileges, Engine,
    Follow that title, nor how swift: today
    When he has put on his lord's face once, then –

FITZDOTTREL. Sir, for these things I shall do well enough,
    There is no fear of me. But then, my wife is   15
    Such an untoward thing! She'll never learn
    How to comport with it! I am out of all
    Conceit on her behalf.

MERECRAFT.   Best have her taught, sir.

FITZDOTTREL. Where? Are there any schools for ladies? Is there
    An academy for women? I do know   20
    For men there was: I learned in it myself
    To make my legs, and do my postures.

    ENGINE *whispers* MERECRAFT.

ENGINE.   Sir.
    Do you remember the conceit you had –
    O' the Spanish gown, at home?

MERECRAFT.   Ha! I do thank thee
    With all my heart, dear Engine.

    MERECRAFT *turns to* FITZDOTTREL.

                    Sir, there is   25
    A certain lady, here about the town,
    An English widow, who hath lately travelled,
    But she's called the Spaniard 'cause she came
    Latest from thence, and keeps the Spanish habit.
    Such a rare woman! All our women here   30
    That are of spirit and fashion flock unto her,
    As to their president, their law, their canon,
    More than they ever did to oracle Forman.

Such rare receipts she has, sir, for the face;
Such oils, such tinctures, such pomatums,   35
Such perfumes, medicines, quintessences, etc.
And such a mistress of behaviour;
She knows, from the duke's daughter to the doxy,
What is their due just, and no more!

FITZDOTTREL.   O sir!
You please me i'this more than mine own greatness.   40
Where is she? Let us have her.

MERECRAFT.   By your patience,
We must use means; cast how to be acquainted –

FITZDOTTREL. Good sir, about it.

MERECRAFT.   We must think how, first.

FITZDOTTREL.   O!
I do not love to tarry for a thing
When I have a mind to't. You do not know me,   45
If you do offer it.

MERECRAFT.   Your wife must send
Some pretty token to her, with a compliment,
And pray to be received in her good graces.
All the great ladies do't –

FITZDOTTREL.   She shall, she shall,
What were it best to be?

MERECRAFT.   Some little toy,   50
I would not have it any great matter, sir:
A diamond ring of forty or fifty pound
Would do it handsomely: and be a gift
Fit for your wife to send, and her to take.

FITZDOTTREL. I'll go and tell my wife on't straight.   54

   FITZDOTTREL *goes out.*

MERECRAFT.   Why this
Is well! The clothes we'have now, but where's this lady?
If we could get a witty boy now, Engine,

That were an excellent crack. I could instruct him
To the true height. For any thing takes this dott'rel.

ENGINE. Why, sir, your best will be one o'the players!   60

MERECRAFT. No, there's no trusting them. They'll talk on't,
    And tell their poets.

ENGINE.   What if they do? The jest
    Will brook the stage. But there be some of 'em
    Are very honest lads. There's Dick Robinson,
    A very pretty fellow, and comes often   65
    To a gentleman's chamber, a friend's of mine. We had
    The merriest supper of it there, one night –
    The gentleman's landlady invited him
    To'a gossips' feast. Now he, sir, brought Dick Robinson
    Dressed like a lawyer's wife, amongst 'em all –   70
    I lent him clothes – but, to see him behave it,
    And lay the law, and carve, and drink unto 'em,
    And then talk bawdy, and send frolics! O!
    It would have burst your buttons, or not left you
    A seam.

MERECRAFT. They say he's an ingenious youth!   75

ENGINE. O sir! And dresses himself the best! Beyond
    Forty o' your very ladies! Did you ne'er see him?

MERECRAFT. No, I do seldom see those toys. But think you
    That we may have him?

ENGINE.   Sir, the young gentleman
    I tell you of, can command him. Shall I attempt it?   80

MERECRAFT. Yes, do it.

    [FITZDOTTREL] *enters again.*

FITZDOTTREL.   'Slight, I cannot get my wife
    To part with a ring on any terms: and yet
    The sullen monkey has two.

MERECRAFT.   It were 'gainst reason
    That you should urge it; sir, send to a goldsmith,

Let her not lose by't.

FITZDOTTREL.   How does she lose by't?   85
Is't not for her?

MERECRAFT.   Make it your own bounty,
It will ha' the better success; what is a matter
Of fifty pound to you, sir?

FITZDOTTREL.   I've but a hundred
Pieces to show here; that I would not break –

MERECRAFT. You shall ha' credit, sir. I'll send a ticket   90
Unto my goldsmith. Here my man comes too,
To carry it fitly.

  TRAINS *enters.*

            How now, Trains? What birds?

TRAINS. Your cousin Everill met me, and has beat me
Because I would not tell him where you were:
I think he has dogged me to the house too.

MERECRAFT.   Well –   95
You shall go out at the back door then, Trains.
You must get Gilthead hither, by some means.

TRAINS. 'Tis impossible!

FITZDOTTREL.   Tell him, we have venison –
I'll gi' him a piece, and send his wife a pheasant.

  [*Exit* FITZDOTTREL.]

TRAINS. A forest moves not till that forty pound   100
You'had of him last be paid. He keeps more stir
For that same petty sum, than for your bond
Of six, and statute of eight hundred!

MERECRAFT.   Tell him
We'll hedge in that. Cry up Fitzdotrel to him,
Double his price, make him a man of metal.   105

TRAINS. That will not need, his bond is current enough.

  [*Exeunt.*]

Act III, Scene i

[*Enter*] GILTHEAD [*and*] PLUTARCHUS.

GILTHEAD. All this is to make you a gentleman;
    I'll have you learn, son. Wherefore have I placed you
    With Sir Paul Eitherside, but to have so much law
    To keep your own? Besides, he is a justice
    Here i' the town; and dwelling, son, with him   5
    You shall learn that in a year, shall be worth twenty
    Of having stayed you at Oxford, or at Cambridge,
    Or sending you to the Inns of Court, or France.
    I am called for now in haste by Master Merecraft
    To trust Master Fitzdottrel, a good man –   10
    I've enquired him, eighteen hundred a year,
    His name is current – for a diamond ring
    Of forty, shall not be worth thirty (that's gained).
    And this is to make you a gentleman!   14

PLUTARCHUS. O, but good father, you trust too much!

GILTHEAD.   Boy, boy,
    We live by finding fools out to be trusted.
    Our shop-books are our pastures, our corn-grounds,
    We lay 'em op'n, for them to come into:
    And when we have 'em there, we drive 'em up
    In to'one of our two pounds, the Counters, straight,   20
    And this is to make you a gentleman!
    We citizens never trust, but we do cozen:
    For if our debtors pay, we cozen them;
    And if they do not, then we cozen ourselves.
    But that's a hazard everyone must run   25
    That hopes to make his son a gentleman!

PLUTARCHUS. I do not wish to be one, truly, father.

In a descent or two we come to be
Just i'their state, fit to be cozened like 'em.
And I had rather ha' tarried i'your trade: 30
For since the gentry scorn the city so much,
Methinks we should in time, holding together,
And matching in our own tribes, as they say,
Have got an Act of Common Council for it,
That we might cozen them out of *rerum natura*.   35

GILTHEAD. Ay, if we had an Act first to forbid
The marrying of our wealthy heirs unto 'em,
And daughters with such lavish portions.
That confounds all.

PLUTARCHUS.   And makes a mongrel breed, father.
And when they have your money, then they laugh at you,   40
Or kick you down the stairs. I cannot abide 'em.
I would fain have 'em cozened, but not trusted.

Act III, Scene ii

[*Enter*] MERECRAFT [*and*] FITZDOTTREL.

MERECRAFT. O, is he come! I knew he would not fail me.
Welcome, good Gilthead, I must ha' you do
A noble gentleman a courtesy here:
In a mere toy, some pretty ring or jewel,
Of fifty or three score pound – make it a hundred,   5
And hedge in the last forty that I owe you,
And your own price for the ring – he's a good man, sir
And you may hap'see him a great one! He
Is likely to bestow hundreds and thousands
Wi' you, if you can humour him. A great prince   10
He will be shortly. What do you say?

GILTHEAD.   In truth, sir,

I cannot. 'T has been a long vacation with us –

FITZDOTTREL. Of what, I pray thee? Of wit? Or honesty?
    Those are your citizens' long vacations.

PLUTARCHUS. Good father, do not trust 'em.

MERECRAFT.   Nay, Thom Gilthead,
    He will not buy a courtesy and beg it: 16
    He'll rather pay than pray. If you do for him,
    You must do cheerfully. His credit, sir,
    Is not yet prostitute! Who's this? Thy son?
    A pretty youth, what's his name?

PLUTARCHUS.   Plutarchus, sir.   20

MERECRAFT. Plutarchus! How came that about?

GILTHEAD.   That year, sir,
    That I begot him, I bought Plutarch's *Lives*,
    And fell so'in love with the book as I called my son
    By'his name, in hope he should be like him
    And write the lives of our great men!

MERECRAFT.   I' the city!   25
    And you do breed him there?

GILTHEAD.   His mind, sir, lies
    Much to that way.

MERECRAFT.   Why then, he is i'the right way.

GILTHEAD. But now I had rather get him a good wife,
    And plant him i'the country; there to use
    The blessing I shall leave him.

MERECRAFT.   Out upon't!   30
    And lose the laudable means thou hast at home, here,
    To'advance and make him a young alderman?
    Buy him a captain's place, for shame; and let him
    Into the world early, and with his plume
    And scarfs, march through Cheapside, or along Cornhill,   35
    And by the virtue'of those, draw down a wife
    There from a window, worth ten thousand pound!

Get him the posture book, and's leaden men
To set upon a table, 'gainst his mistress
Chance to come by, that he may draw her in   40
And show her Finsbury battles.

GILTHEAD.   I have placed him
  With Justice Eitherside, to get so much law –

MERECRAFT. As thou hast conscience. Come, come, thou dost
    wrong
  Pretty Plutarchus, who had not his name
  For nothing, but was born to train the youth   45
  Of London in the military truth –
  That way his genius lies. My cousin Everill!

Act III, Scene iii

[*Enter*] EVERILL.

EVERILL. O, are you here, sir? Pray you let us whisper.

  [*Takes* MERECRAFT *aside.*]

PLUTARCHUS. Father, dear father, trust him if you love me.

GILTHEAD. Why, I do mean it, boy; but what I do
  Must not come easily from me: we must deal
  With courtiers, boy, as courtiers deal with us.   5
  If I have a business there with any of them,
  Why I must wait, I'm sure on't, son: and though
  My lord dispatch me, yet his worshipful man
  Will keep me for his sport a month, or two,
  To show me with my fellow citizens.   10
  I must make his train long and full, one quarter;
  And help the spectacle of his greatness. There

Nothing is done at once, but injuries, boy:
And they come headlong! All their good turns move not,
Or very slowly.

PLUTARCHUS.   Yet sweet father, trust him.   15

GILTHEAD. Well, I will think.

[GILTHEAD *and* PLUTARCHUS *walk aside.*]

EVERILL.   Come, you must do't, sir.
I'm undone else, and your Lady Tailbush
Has sent for me to dinner, and my clothes
Are all at pawn. I had sent out this morning,
Before I heard you were come to town, some twenty   20
Of my epistles, and no one return –

MERECRAFT *tells him of his faults.*

MERECRAFT. Why I ha' told you o' this. This comes of wearing
Scarlet, gold lace, and cut-works! Your fine gartering!
With your blown roses, cousin! And your eating
Pheasant, and godwit, here in London! Haunting   25
The Globes and Mermaids! wedging in with lords
Still at the table! and affecting lechery
In velvet! Where could you ha' contented yourself
With cheese, salt-butter, and a pickled herring,
I'the Low Countries? There worn cloth, and fustian!   30
Been satisfied with a leap o' your host's daughter,
In garrison, a wench of a stoter! Or
Your sutler's wife, i'the leaguer, of two blanks!
You never, then, had run upon this flat,
To write your letters missive and send out   35
Your privy seals, that thus have frighted off
All your acquaintance; that they shun you at distance
Worse than you do the bailies!

EVERILL.   Pox upon you.

He repines.

I come not to you for counsel, I lack money.

MERECRAFT. You do not think what you owe me already?

EVERILL.   I?   40
    They owe you that mean to pay you. I'll be sworn,
    I never meant it. Come, you will project:
    I shall undo your practice for this month else:
    You know me.

    And threatens him.

MERECRAFT.   Ay, you're a right sweet nature!

EVERILL. Well, that's all one!

MERECRAFT.   You'll leave this empire one day!   45
    You will not ever have this tribute paid,
    Your sceptre o' the sword!

EVERILL.   Tie up your wit,
    Do, and provoke me not –

MERECRAFT.   Will you, sir, help
    To what I shall provoke another for you?

EVERILL. I cannot tell; try me. I think I am not   50
    So utterly of an ore un-to-be-melted
    But I can do myself good, on occasions.

MERECRAFT. Strike in then, for your part.

    They join.

                                        Master Fitzdottrel,
    If I transgress in point of manners, afford me
    Your best construction; I must beg my freedom   55
    From your affairs this day.

    MERECRAFT *pretends business.*

FITZDOTTREL.   How, sir?

MERECRAFT.   It is
    In succour of this gentleman's occasions,
    My kinsman –

FITZDOTTREL. You'll not do me that affront, sir.

MERECRAFT. I am sorry you should so interpret it,
 But, sir, it stands upon his being invested   60
 In a new office he has stood for, long:

 MERECRAFT *describes the Office of Dependancy.*

 Master of the Dependances! A place
 Of my projection too, sir, and hath met
 Much opposition; but the State now sees
 That great necessity of it, as after all   65
 Their writing and their speaking against duels,
 They have erected it. His book is drawn –
 For since there will be differences daily
 'Twixt gentlemen, and that the roaring manner
 Is grown offensive, that those few, we call   70
 The civil men o' the sword, abhor the vapours,
 They shall refer now, hither, for their process:
 And such as trespass 'gainst the rule of court,
 Are to be fined –

FITZDOTTREL. In troth, a pretty place!

MERECRAFT. A kind of arbitrary court 'twill be, sir.   75

FITZDOTTREL. I shall have matter for it, I believe,
 Ere it be long: I had a distaste.

MERECRAFT.   But now, sir,
 My learned counsel, they must have a feeling;
 They'll part, sir, with no books without the hand-gout
 Be oiled, and I must furnish. If 't be money,   80
 To me straight. I am mine, mint and exchequer,
 To supply all. What is't? A hundred pound?

EVERILL. No, the' harpy now stands on a hundred pieces.

MERECRAFT. Why he must have 'em if he will. Tomorrow, sir,
 Will equally serve your occasions,   85
 And therefore let me obtain that you will yield
 To timing a poor gentleman's distresses,
 In terms of hazard –

FITZDOTTREL. By no means!

MERECRAFT.   I must
   Get him this money, and will –

FITZDOTTREL.   Sir, I protest
   I'd rather stand engaged for it myself,   90
   Than you should leave me.

MERECRAFT.   O good sir, do you think
   So coarsely of our manners that we would,
   For any need of ours, be pressed to take it
   Though you be pleased to offer it?

FITZDOTTREL.   Why, by heaven,
   I mean it!

MERECRAFT. I can never believe less.   95
   But we, sir, must preserve our dignity,
   As you do publish yours. By your fair leave, sir.

He offers to be gone.

FITZDOTTREL. As I am a gentleman, if you do offer
   To leave me now, or if you do refuse me,
   I will not think you love me.

MERECRAFT.   Sir, I honour you.   100
   And with just reason, for these noble notes
   Of the nobility you pretend to! But sir,
   I would know why! A motive – he a stranger –
   You should do this?

EVERILL [*aside*].   You'll mar all with your fineness.   104

FITZDOTTREL. Why that's all one if 'twere, sir, but my fancy.
   But I have a business that perhaps I'd have
   Brought to his office.

MERECRAFT.   O, sir! I have done then;
   If he can be made profitable to you.

FITZDOTTREL. Yes, and it shall be one of my ambitions
   To have it the first business. May I not?   110

EVERILL. So you do mean to make't a perfect business.

FITZDOTTREL. Nay, I'll do that, assure you: show me once.

MERECRAFT. Sir, it concerns the first be a perfect business
    For his own honour!

EVERILL.   Ay, and the'reputation
    Too, of my place.

FITZDOTTREL.   Why, why do I take this course else?   115
    I am not altogether an ass, good gentleman,
    Wherefore should I consult you? Do you think
    To make a song on't? How's your manner? Tell us.

MERECRAFT. Do, satisfy him: give him the whole course.

EVERILL. First, by request, or otherwise, you offer   120
    Your business to the court: wherein you crave
    The judgement of the Master and the Assistants.

FITZDOTTREL. Well, that's done, now what do you upon it?

EVERILL. We straight, sir, have recourse to the spring-head;
    Visit the ground and so disclose the nature,   125
    If it will carry, or no. If we do find,
    By our proportions it is like to prove
    A sullen, and black business, that it be
    Incorrigible and out of treaty, then
    We file it a dependance!

FITZDOTTREL.   So, 'tis filed.   130
    What follows? I do love the order of these things.

EVERILL. We then advise the party, if he be
    A man of means and havings, that forthwith
    He settle his estate: if not, at least
    That he pretend it. For by that the world   135
    Takes notice that it now is a dependance.
    And this we call, sir, publication.

FITZDOTTREL. Very sufficient! After publication, now?

EVERILL. Then we grant out our process, which is divers;
    Either by chartel, sir, or ore-tenus,   140
    Wherein the challenger and challengee,

Or – with your Spaniard – your *provocador*
And *provocado*, have their several courses –

FITZDOTTREL. I have enough on't! For an hundred pieces?
    Yes, for two hundred underwrite me, do.   145
    Your man will take my bond?

MERECRAFT.   That he will, sure,
    But these same citizens, they are such sharks!

He whispers [with] FITZDOTTREL, *aside.*

    There's an old debt of forty, I ga' my word
    For one is run away to the Bermudas,
    And he will hook in that, or he will'not do.   150

FITZDOTTREL. Why let him. That and the ring, and a hundred
        pieces,
    Will all but make two hundred?

MERECRAFT.   No, no more, sir.
    What ready arithmetic you have!

And then [he whispers to] GILTHEAD.

                 Do you hear?
    A pretty morning's work for you, this? Do it,
    You shall ha' twenty pound on't.

GILTHEAD.   Twenty pieces?   155

PLUTARCHUS. Good father, do't.

MERECRAFT. You will hook still? well,
    Show us your ring. You could not ha' done this, now
    With gentleness at first, we might ha' thanked you?
    But groan, and ha' your courtesies come from you
    Like a hard stool, and stink? A man may draw   160
    Your teeth out easier than your money! Come,
    Were little Gilthead here, no better a nature,

He pulls PLUTARCHUS *by the lips.*

I should ne'er love him, that could pull his lips off, now!
Was not thy mother a gentlewoman?

PLUTARCHUS.   Yes, sir.

MERECRAFT. And went to the Court at Christmas, and St
    George's tide?   165
  And lent the lords' men chains?

PLUTARCHUS.   Of gold, and pearl, sir.

MERECRAFT. I knew thou must take after somebody!
  Thou couldst not be else. This was no shop-look!
  I'll ha' thee Captain Gilthead, and march up,
  And take in Pimlico, and kill the bush   170
  At every tavern! Thou shalt have a wife,
  If smocks will mount, boy.

He turns to old GILTHEAD.

                How now? You ha' there now
Some Bristol-stone, or Cornish counterfeit
You'd put upon us.

GILTHEAD.   No sir, I assure you:
  Look on his lustre! He will speak himself!   175
  I'll gi' you leave to put him i' the mill,
  He's no great, large stone, but a true paragon,
  He'has all his corners, view him well.

MERECRAFT.   He's yellow.

GILTHEAD. Upon'my faith, sir, o' the right black water,
  And very deep! He's set without a foil, too.   180
  Here's one o' the yellow water, I'll sell cheap.

MERECRAFT. And what do you value this at? Thirty pound?

GILTHEAD. No sir, he cost me forty, ere he was set.

MERECRAFT. Turnings, you mean? I know your equivoques:
  You're grown the better fathers of 'em o'late.   185
  Well, where't must go, 'twill be judged, and therefore
  Look you't be right. You shall have fifty pound for't.
  Not a denier more!

Now to FITZDOTTREL.

And because you would
Have things dispatched, sir, I'll go presently
Enquire out this lady. If you think good, sir,   190
Having an hundred pieces ready, you may
Part with those now to serve my kinsman's turns,
That he may wait upon you anon the freer;
And take 'em when you ha' sealed again of Gilthead.

FITZDOTTREL. I care not if I do!

MERECRAFT.   And dispatch all   195
Together.

FITZDOTTREL. There, they're just: a hundred pieces!
I ha' told 'em over, twice a day, these two months.

MERECRAFT. Well go and seal then, sir, make your return
As speedy as you can.

He turns 'em out together. And EVERILL *and* [MERECRAFT] *fall to share.*

EVERILL.   Come gi' me.

MERECRAFT.   Soft, sir –

EVERILL. Marry, and fair too then. I'll no delaying, sir.   200

MERECRAFT. But you will hear?

EVERILL.   Yes, when I have my dividend.

MERECRAFT. There's forty pieces for you.

EVERILL.   What is this for?

MERECRAFT. Your half. You know that Gilthead must ha' twenty.

EVERILL. And what's your ring there? Shall I ha' none o' that?

MERECRAFT. O, that's to be given to a lady!   205

EVERILL. Is't so?

MERECRAFT.   By that good light, it is.

EVERILL.   Come, gi' me
Ten pieces more, then.

MERECRAFT.   Why?

EVERILL.   For Gilthead? Sir,
  Do'you think I'll 'low him any such share?

MERECRAFT.   You must.

EVERILL. Must I? Do you your musts, sir, I'll do mine.
  You wi' not part with the whole, sir? Will you? Go to.   210
  Gi' me ten pieces!

MERECRAFT.   By what law, do you this?

EVERILL. E'en lion-law, sir; I must roar else.

MERECRAFT.   Good!

EVERILL. You've heard how the'ass made his divisions wisely?

MERECRAFT. And I am he: I thank you.

EVERILL.   Much good do you, sir.

MERECRAFT. I shall be rid o' this tyranny, one day!

EVERILL.   Not   215
  While you do eat, and lie about the town here,
  And cozen i' your bullions, and I stand
  Your name of credit, and compound your business,
  Adjourn your beatings every term, and make
  New parties for your projects. I have now   220
  A pretty task of it, to hold you in
  Wi' your Lady Tailbush: but the toy will be
  How we shall both come off?

MERECRAFT.   Leave you your doubting.
  And do your portion, what's assigned you: I
  Never failed yet.

EVERILL.   With reference to your aids?   225
  You'll still be unthankful. Where shall I meet you, anon?
  You ha' some feat to do alone now, I see;
  You wish me gone; well I will find you out,
  And bring you after to the audit.

  [*Exit.*]

MERECRAFT.   'Slight!
   There's Engine's share too, I had forgot! This reign   230
   Is too-too-unsupportable! I must
   Quit myself of this vassalage! Engine! Welcome.

Act III, Scene iv

[*Enter*] ENGINE [*and*] WITTIPOL.

MERECRAFT. How goes the cry?

ENGINE.   Excellent well!

MERECRAFT.   Will't do?
   Where's Robinson?

ENGINE.   Here is the gentleman, sir,
   Will undertake't himself. I have acquainted him.

MERECRAFT. Why did you so?

ENGINE.   Why Robinson would ha' told him,
   You know. And he's a pleasant wit! Will hurt   5
   Nothing you purpose. Then, he's of opinion
   That Robinson might want audacity,
   She being such a gallant. Now he has been
   In Spain, and knows the fashions there, and can
   Discourse; and being but mirth, he says, leave much   10
   To his care.

MERECRAFT. But he is too tall!

He excepts at his stature.

ENGINE.   For that
   He has the bravest device! – You'll love him for't –
   To say he wears cioppinos, and they do so
   In Spain. And Robinson's as tall as he.

MERECRAFT. Is he so?

ENGINE.   Every jot.

MERECRAFT.   Nay, I had rather   15
  To trust a gentleman with it, o' the two.

ENGINE. Pray you go to him then, sir, and salute him.

MERECRAFT. Sir, my friend Engine has acquainted you
  With a strange business here.

WITTIPOL.   A merry one, sir.
  The Duke of Drowned-land, and his Duchess?

MERECRAFT.   Yes, sir.   20
  Now that the conjurers ha' laid him by,
  I ha' made bold to borrow him a while –

WITTIPOL. With purpose yet to put him out, I hope,
  To his best use?

MERECRAFT.   Yes, sir.

WITTIPOL.   For that small part
  That I am trusted with, put off your care: 25
  I would not lose to do it for the mirth
  Will follow of it, and well, I have a fancy.

MERECRAFT. Sir, that will make it well.

WITTIPOL.   You will report it so.
  Where must I have my dressing?

ENGINE.   At my house, sir.

MERECRAFT. You shall have caution, sir, for what he yields   30
  To sixpence.

WITTIPOL.   You shall pardon me. I will share, sir,
  I' your sports only: nothing i' your purchase.
  But you must furnish me with complements,
  To th' manner of Spain; my coach, my guarda-duennas –

MERECRAFT. Engine's your provedor. But sir, I must –   35
  Now I've entered trust wi'you thus far –

Secure still i' your quality, acquaint you
With somewhat beyond this. The place designed
To be the scene for this our merry matter,
Because it must have countenance of women   40
To draw discourse and offer it, is here by,
At the Lady Tailbush's.

WITTIPOL.   I know her, sir,
And her gentleman usher.

MERECRAFT.   Master Ambler?

WITTIPOL.   Yes, sir.

MERECRAFT. Sir, it shall be no shame to me to confess
To you that we poor gentlemen that want acres,   45
Must for our needs turn fools up, and plough ladies
Sometimes to try what glebe they are: and this
Is no unfruitful piece. She and I now
Are on a project for the fact, and venting
Of a new kind of fucus (paint, for ladies)   50
To serve the kingdom: wherein she herself
Hath travailed specially by way of service
Unto her sex, and hopes to get the monopoly
As the reward, of her invention.

WITTIPOL. What is her end in this?

MERECRAFT.   Merely ambition,   55
Sir, to grow great, and court it with the secret,
Though she pretend some other. For she's dealing
Already upon caution for the shares;
And Master Ambler, is he named examiner
For the ingredients, and the register   60
Of what is vented, and shall keep the office.
Now if she break with you of this – as I
Must make the leading thread to your acquaintance,
That how experience gotten i' your being
Abroad will help our business – think of some   65
Pretty additions but to keep her floating:
It may be she will offer you a part,

Any strange names of –

WITTIPOL.   Sir, I have my'instructions.
   Is it not high time to be making ready?   69

MERECRAFT. Yes, sir.

ENGINE.   The fool's in sight, Dott'rel.

MERECRAFT.   Away, then.

   [*Exeunt* WITTIPOL *and* ENGINE.]

Act III, Scene v

[*Enter*] FITZDOTTREL.

[MERECRAFT]. Returned so soon?

FITZDOTTREL.   Yes, here's the ring: I ha' sealed.
   But there's not so much gold in all the row, he says –
   Till 't come fro' the Mint. 'Tis ta'en up for the gamesters.

MERECRAFT. There's a shop-shift! Plague on 'em.

FITZDOTTREL.   He does swear it.

MERECRAFT. He'll swear and forswear too, it is his trade;   5
   You should not have left him.

FITZDOTTREL.   'Slid, I can go back
   And beat him, yet.

MERECRAFT.   No, now let him alone.

FITZDOTTREL. I was so earnest after the main business,
   To have this ring gone.

MERECRAFT.   True, and 'tis time.
   I've learned, sir, sin' you went, her ladyship eats   10
   With the Lady Tailbush here, hard by.

FITZDOTTREL.   I' the lane here?

MERECRAFT. Yes, if you'd a servant now of presence,
    Well clothed, and of an airy voluble tongue,
    Neither too big or little for his mouth,
    That could deliver your wife's compliment,   15
    To send along withal.

FITZDOTTREL.   I have one sir,
    A very handsome, gentleman-like fellow,
    That I do mean to make my duchess' usher –
    I entertained him but this morning too:
    I'll call him to you. The worst of him is his name!   20

MERECRAFT. She'll take no note of that, but of his message.

FITZDOTTREL. Devil!

He shows him his PUG.

                    How like you him, sir? Pace, go a little.
    Let's see you move.

MERECRAFT.   He'll serve, sir, give it him:
    And let him go along with me, I'll help
    To present him, and it.

FITZDOTTREL.   Look you do, sirrah,   25
    Discharge this well, as you expect your place.
    Do'you hear, go on, come off with all your honours.
    I would fain see him do it.

MERECRAFT.   Trust him with it.

FITZDOTTREL [*gives him instructions*].
    Remember kissing of your hand, and answering
    With the French-time, in flexure of your body.   30
    I could now so instruct him – and for his words –

MERECRAFT. I'll put them in his mouth.

FITZDOTTREL.   O, but I have 'em
    O' the very academies.

MERECRAFT.   Sir, you'll have use for 'em

Anon, yourself, I warrant you: after dinner,
When you are called.

FITZDOTTREL.   'Slight, that'll be just play-time.   35

He longs to see the play. . .

It cannot be, I must not lose the play!

MERECRAFT. Sir, but you must if she appoint to sit. And she's
    president.

FITZDOTTREL. 'Slid, it is 'The Devil'!

. . . because it is 'The Devil'.

MERECRAFT. And 'twere his dam too, you must now apply
Yourself, sir, to this wholly or lose all.   40

FITZDOTTREL. If I could but see a piece –

MERECRAFT.   Sir, never think on't.

FITZDOTTREL. Come but to one act, and I did not care –
But to be seen to rise, and go away,
To vex the players, and to punish their poet –
Keep him in awe!

MERECRAFT.   But say that he be one   45
Wi' not be awed, but laugh at you. How then?

FITZDOTTREL. Then he shall pay for'his dinner himself.

MERECRAFT.   Perhaps,
He would do that twice, rather than thank you.
Come, get 'The Devil' out of your head, my lord –
I'll call you so in private still – and take   50
Your lordship i' your mind.

He puts him in mind of his quarrel.

               You were, sweet lord,
In talk to bring a business to the office.

FITZDOTTREL.   Yes.

MERECRAFT. Why should not you, sir, carry it o' yourself,

Before the office be up? And show the world
You had no need of any man's direction;   55
In point, sir, of sufficiency. I speak
Against a kinsman, but as one that tenders
Your grace's good.

FITZDOTTREL.   I thank you; to proceed –

MERECRAFT. To publications: ha' your deed drawn presently,
And leave a blank to put in your feoffees,   60
One, two, or more, as you see cause –

FITZDOTTREL.   I thank you
Heartily, I do thank you. Not a word more,
I pray you, as you love me. Let me alone.

He is angry with himself.

That I could not think o'this, as well, as he!
O, I could beat my infinite blockhead – !   65

[*Exit* FITZDOTTREL.]

MERECRAFT. Come, we must this way.

PUG.   How far is't?

MERECRAFT.   Hard by here
Over the way. Now, to achieve this ring
From this same fellow, that is to assure it
Before he give it.

He thinks how to cozen the bearer of the ring.

                    Though my Spanish lady
Be a young gentleman of means, and scorn   70
To share as he doth say, I do not know
How such a toy may tempt his ladyship:
And therefore, I think best, it be assured.

PUG. Sir, be the ladies brave, we go unto?

MERECRAFT. O yes.

PUG.   And shall I see 'em, and speak to 'em?   75

MERECRAFT. What else?

　　[*Enter* TRAINS.] *Questions his man.*

　　　　　　　　Ha' you your false beard about you, Trains?

TRAINS. Yes.

MERECRAFT. And is this one of your double cloaks?

TRAINS. The best of 'em.

MERECRAFT.　　　　　　Be ready then.

　　[*Exit* TRAINS. *Enter* PITFALL.]

　　　　　　　　　　　　　　Sweet Pitfall!

Act III, Scene vi

MERECRAFT. Come, I must buss

　　Offers to kiss.

PITFALL.　　　　　　　　　Away.

MERECRAFT.　　　　　　　　　　I'll set thee up again.
　　Never fear that: canst thou get ne'er a bird?
　　No thrushes hungry? Stay till cold weather come,
　　I'll help thee to an ousel, or a fieldfare.
　　Who's within, with madam?

PITFALL.　　　　　　　　I'll tell you straight.　　　　　5

　　She runs in, in haste.

MERECRAFT. Please you stay here a while, sir, I'll go in.

　　He follows.

PUG. I do so long to have a little venery,
　　While I am in this body! I would taste
　　Of every sin a little, if it might be

After the manner of man!

[*Enter* PITFALL.] PUG *leaps at* PITFALL's *coming in.*

                              Sweetheart!

PITFALL.   What would you, sir?   10

PUG. Nothing but fall in, to you, be your blackbird,
  My pretty pit (as the gentleman said) your throstle:
  Lie tame, and taken with you; here's gold!
  To buy you so much new stuffs from the shop,
  As I may take the old up –

  TRAINS *in his false cloak brings a false message, and gets the ring.*

TRAINS.   You must send, sir,   15
  The gentleman the ring.

PUG.   There 'tis.

  [*Exit* TRAINS *with the ring.*]
                              Nay look,
  Will you be foolish, Pit?

PITFALL.   This is strange rudeness.

PUG. Dear Pit.

PITFALL.   I 'll call, I swear.

  [*Exit.*] MERECRAFT *follows presently, and asks for* [*the ring*].

MERECRAFT [*within*].   Where are you, sir?
  Is your ring ready? Go with me.

PUG.   I sent it you.

MERECRAFT. Me? When? By whom?

PUG.   A fellow here, e'en now,   20
  Came for it i' your name.

MERECRAFT.   I sent none, sure.
  My meaning ever was you should deliver it
  Yourself: so was your master's charge, you know.
  What fellow was it, do you know him?

PUG.   Here,
  But now, he had it.

  Enter TRAINS *as himself again.*

MERECRAFT.   Saw you any, Trains?   25

TRAINS. Not I.

PUG.   The gentlewoman saw him.

MERECRAFT.   Enquire.

  [*Exit* TRAINS.] *The* DEVIL *confesseth himself cozened.*

PUG. I was so earnest upon her, I marked not!
  My devilish chief has put me here in flesh,
  To shame me! This dull body I am in,
  I perceive nothing with! I offer at nothing   30
  That will succeed!

  [*Enter* TRAINS.]

TRAINS.   Sir, she saw none, she says.

PUG. Satan himself has ta'en a shape to'abuse me.
  It could not be else!

MERECRAFT.   This is above strange!

  MERECRAFT *accuseth him of negligence.*

  That you should be so wretchless! What'll you do, sir?
  How will you answer this when you are questioned?   35

PUG. Run from my flesh if I could: put off mankind!
  This's such a scorn! And will be a new exercise
  For my archduke! Woe to the several cudgels
  Must suffer on this back! Can you no succours? Sir?

  He asketh aid.

MERECRAFT. Alas! The use of it is so present.

PUG.   I ask,   40
  Sir, credit for another but till tomorrow!

MERECRAFT. There is not so much time, sir. But however

The lady is a noble lady, and will –
To save a gentleman from check – be entreated
To say she has received it.

PUG.   Do you think so?   45
Will she be won?

  MERECRAFT *promiseth faintly, yet comforts him.*

MERECRAFT.   No doubt, to such an office,
It will be a lady's bravery and her pride.

PUG. And not be known on't after unto him?

MERECRAFT. That were a treachery! Upon my word,
Be confident. Return unto your master,   50
My lady president sits this afternoon;
Has ta'en the ring, commends her services
Unto your lady duchess. You may say
She's a civil lady, and does give her
All her respects already: bade you tell her   55
She lives but to receive her wished commandments,
And have the honour here to kiss her hands:
For which she'll stay this hour yet. Hasten you
Your prince, away.

  The DEVIL *is doubtful.*

PUG.   And sir, you will take care
The'excuse be perfect?

MERECRAFT.   You confess your fears   60
Too much.

PUG.   The shame is more.

MERECRAFT.   I'll quit you of either.

  [*Exeunt.*]

Act IV, Scene i

[*Enter* LADY] TAILBUSH [*and*] MERECRAFT.

TAILBUSH. A pox upo' referring to commissioners,
    I'd rather hear that it were past the seals:
    Your courtiers move so snail-like i' your business.
    Would I had not begun wi' you.

MERECRAFT.   We must move,
    Madam, in order, by degrees: not jump.   5

TAILBUSH. Why, there was Sir John Moneyman could jump
    A business quickly.

MERECRAFT.   True, he had great friends,
    But because some, sweet madam, can leap ditches,
    We must not all shun to go over bridges.
    The harder parts, I make account, are done,   10
    Now,'tis referred.

He flatters her.

                 You are infinitely bound
    Unto the ladies, they ha' so cried it up!

TAILBUSH. Do they like it then?

MERECRAFT.   They ha' sent the Spanish lady
    To gratulate with you –

TAILBUSH.   I must send 'em thanks
    And some remembrances.

MERECRAFT.   That you must, and visit 'em.   15
    Where's Ambler?

TAILBUSH.   Lost, today we cannot hear of him.

MERECRAFT. Not, madam?

TAILBUSH.   No in good faith. They say he lay not
    At home tonight. And here has fallen a business
    Between your cousin and Master Manly has
    Unquieted us all.

MERECRAFT.   So I hear, madam.   20
    Pray you, how was it?

TAILBUSH.   Troth, it but appears
    Ill o' your kinsman's part. You may have heard
    That Manly is a suitor to me, I doubt not –

MERECRAFT. I guessed it, madam.

TAILBUSH.   And it seems he trusted
    Your cousin to let fall some fair reports   25
    Of him unto me.

MERECRAFT.   Which he did!

TAILBUSH.   So far
    From it, as he came in and took him railing
    Against him.

MERECRAFT.   How! And what said Manly to him?

TAILBUSH. Enough, I do assure you: and with that scorn
    Of him and the injury, as I do wonder   30
    How Everill bore it! But that guilt undoes
    Many men's valours.

MERECRAFT.   Here comes Manly.

    [*Enter* MANLY.]

MANLY.   Madam,
    I'll take my leave

    MANLY *offers to be gone.*

TAILBUSH. You sha'not go, i' faith.
    I'll ha'you stay and see this Spanish miracle
    Of our English lady.

MANLY.   Let me pray your ladyship,   35
    Lay your commands on me some other time.

TAILBUSH. Now, I protest: and I will have all pieced,
    And friends again.

MANLY.   It will be but ill soldered!

TAILBUSH. You are too much affected with it.

MANLY.   I cannot,
    Madam, but think on't for the' injustice.

TAILBUSH.   Sir,   40
    His kinsman here is sorry.

    MERECRAFT *denies him.*

MERECRAFT.   Not I, madam,
    I am no kin to him, we but call cousins,
    And if we were, sir, I have no relation
    Unto his crimes.

MANLY.   You are not urged with 'em.
    I can accuse, sir, none but mine own judgement,   45
    For though it were his crime so to betray me,
    I am sure 'twas more mine own, at all to trust him.
    But he therein did use but his old manners,
    And savour strongly what he was before.

TAILBUSH. Come, he will change!

MANLY.   Faith, I must never think it.   50
    Nor were it reason in me to expect
    That for my sake he should put off a nature
    He sucked in with his milk. It may be, madam,
    Deceiving trust is all he has to trust to:
    If so, I shall be loth that any hope   55
    Of mine should bate him of his means.

TAILBUSH.   You're sharp, sir.
    This act may make him honest!

MANLY.   If he were
    To be made honest by an act of parliament
    I should not alter i'my faith of him.

[*Enter* LADY EITHERSIDE.]

TAILBUSH [*spies the* LADY EITHERSIDE]. Eitherside!
    Welcome, dear Eitherside! How hast thou done, good wench? 60
    Thou hast been a stranger! I ha' not seen thee this week.

Act IV, Scene ii

EITHERSIDE. Ever your servant, madam.

TAILBUSH.   Where hast'thou been?
    I did so long to see thee.

EITHERSIDE.   Visiting, and so tired!
    I protest, madam, 'tis a monstrous trouble!

TAILBUSH. And so it is. I swear I must, tomorrow
    Begin my visits – would they were over – at Court.   5
    It tortures me to think on'em.

EITHERSIDE.   I do hear
    You ha' cause, madam, your suit goes on.

TAILBUSH.   Who told thee?

EITHERSIDE. One that can tell: Master Eitherside.

TAILBUSH.   O, thy husband!
    Yes, faith, there's life in't now: it is referred.
    If we once see it under the seals, wench, then   10
    Have with 'em for the great caroche, six horses,
    And the two coachmen, with my Ambler bare,
    And my three women: we will live, i' faith,
    The examples o' the town, and govern it.
    I'll lead the fashion still.

EITHERSIDE.   You do that now,   15
    Sweet madam.

TAILBUSH.   O, but then, I'll every day
    Bring up some new device. Thou and I, Eitherside,
    Will first be in it, I will give it thee;
    And they shall follow us. Thou shalt, I swear,
    Wear every month a new gown out of it.   20

EITHERSIDE. Thank you, good madam.

TAILBUSH.   Pray thee call me Tailbush,
    As I thee, Eitherside; I not love this 'madam'.

EITHERSIDE. Then I protest to you, Tailbush, I am glad
    Your business so succeeds.

TAILBUSH.   Thank thee, good Eitherside.

EITHERSIDE. But Master Eitherside tells me that he likes   25
    Your other business better.

TAILBUSH.   Which?

EITHERSIDE.   O'the toothpicks.

TAILBUSH. I never heard on't.

EITHERSIDE.   Ask Master Merecraft.

    MERECRAFT *hath whispered with* [MANLY] *the while.*

MERECRAFT. Madam? He's one, in a word, I'll trust his malice
    With any man's credit I would have abused!

MANLY. Sir, if you think you do please me in this   30
    You are deceived!

MERECRAFT.   No, but because my lady
    Named him my kinsman I would satisfy you
    What I think of him: and pray you, upon it
    To judge me!

MANLY.   So I do: that ill men's friendship
    Is as unfaithful as themselves.

TAILBUSH.   Do you hear?   35
    Ha' you a business about toothpicks?

MERECRAFT.   Yes, madam.

Did I ne'er tell't you? I meant to have offered it
Your ladyship on the perfecting the patent.

TAILBUSH. How is't?

The Project for Toothpicks.

MERECRAFT.   For serving the whole state with toothpicks;
    Somewhat an intricate business to discourse, but –   40
    I show how much the subject is abused
    First in that one commodity! Then what diseases
    And putrefactions in the gums are bred
    By those are made' of'adulterate and false wood!
    My plot for reformation of these follows: 45
    To have all toothpicks brought unto an office,
    There sealed; and such as counterfeit 'em, mulcted.
    And last, for venting 'em, to have a book
    Printed to teach their use, which every child
    Shall have throughout the kingdom that can read   50
    And learn to pick his teeth by. Which beginning
    Early to practise, with some other rules,
    Of never sleeping with the mouth open, chawing
    Some grains of mastic, will preserve the breath
    Pure, and so free from taint –

[*Enter* TRAINS.]

                  Ha' what is't? Say'st thou?   55

TRAINS *his man whispers him.*

TAILBUSH. Good faith, it sounds a very pretty business!

EITHERSIDE. So Master Eitherside says, madam.

MERECRAFT.   The lady is come.

TAILBUSH. Is she? Good, wait upon her in.

    [*Exit* MERECRAFT.]

                   My Ambler

Was never so ill absent. Eitherside,
How do I look today? Am I not dressed   60

Spruntly?

She looks in her glass.

EITHERSIDE. Yes, verily, madam.

TAILBUSH.   Pox o' madam,
  Will you not leave that?

EITHERSIDE.   Yes, good Tailbush.

TAILBUSH.   So?
  Sounds not that better? What vile fucus is this
  Thou hast got on?

EITHERSIDE.   'Tis pearl.

TAILBUSH.   Pearl? Oyster-shells:
  As I breathe, Eitherside, I know't. Here comes,   65
  They say, a wonder, sirrah, has been in Spain!
  Will teach us all! She's sent to me from Court
  To gratulate with me! Prithee, let's observe her,
  What faults she has, that we may laugh at 'em,
  When she is gone.

EITHERSIDE.   That we will heartily, Tailbush.   70

  WITTIPOL *enters.*

TAILBUS. O me! The very infanta of the giants!

Act IV, Scene iii

[*Enter*] MERECRAFT [*and*] WITTIPOL [*who*] *is dressed like
a Spanish lady.*

MERECRAFT. Here is a noble lady, madam, come
  From your great friends at Court to see your ladyship,
  And have the honour of your acquaintance.

TAILBUSH.   Sir,

She does us honour.

WITTIPOL.   Pray you, say to her ladyship   5
It is the manner of Spain to embrace only,
Never to kiss.

Excuses himself for not kissing.

                    She will excuse the custom!

TAILBUSH. Your use of it is law. Please you, sweet madam,
    To take a seat.

WITTIPOL.   Yes, madam. I've had
    The favour through a world of fair report
    To know your virtues, madam; and in that   10
    Name, have desired the happiness of presenting
    My service to your ladyship!

TAILBUSH.   Your love, madam,
    I must not own it else.

WITTIPOL.   Both are due, madam,
    To your great undertakings.

TAILBUSH.   Great? In troth, madam,
    They are my friends that think 'em anything: 15
    If I can do my sex by 'em any service
    I've my ends, madam.

WITTIPOL.   And they are noble ones,
    That make a multitude beholden, madam:
    The commonwealth of ladies must acknowledge from you.   19

EITHERSIDE. Except some envious, madam.

WITTIPOL.   You're right in that, madam,
    Of which race I encountered some but lately,
    Who, 't seems, have studied reasons to discredit
    Your business.

TAILBUSH.   How, sweet madam?

WITTIPOL.   Nay, the parties
    Will'not be worth your pause – most ruinous things, madam,

That have put off all hope of being recovered   25
To a degree of handsomeness.

TAILBUSH.   But their reasons, madam?
I would fain hear.

WITTIPOL.   Some, madam, I remember.
They say that painting quite destroys the face –

EITHERSIDE. O, that's an old one, madam.

WITTIPOL.   There are new ones, too:
Corrupts the breath; hath left so little sweetness   30
In kissing, as 'tis now used but for fashion,
And shortly will be taken for a punishment;
Decays the fore-teeth that should guard the tongue;
And suffers that run riot everlasting!
And, which is worse, some ladies when they meet   35
Cannot be merry and laugh, but they do spit
In one another's faces!

MANLY *begins to know him.*

MANLY.   I should know
This voice and face too.

WITTIPOL.   Then they say, 'tis dangerous
To all the fallen yet well disposed mad-dames,
That are industrious and desire to earn   40
Their living with their sweat! For any distemper
Of heat and motion may displace the colours;
And if the paint once run about their faces,
Twenty to one they will appear so ill-favoured
Their servants run away, too, and leave the pleasure   45
Imperfect, and the reckoning also'unpaid.

EITHERSIDE. Pox, these are poets' reasons.

TAILBUSH.   Some old lady
That keeps a poet has devised these scandals.

EITHERSIDE. Faith we must have the poets banished, madam,
As Master Eitherside says.

MERECRAFT.   Master Fitzdottrel!   50
  And his wife: where? Madam, the Duke of Drowned-land,
  That will be shortly.

WITTIPOL.   Is this my lord?

MERECRAFT.   The same.

Act IV, Scene iv

[*Enter*] FITZDOTTREL, MISTRESS FITZDOTTREL [*and*] PUG.

FITZDOTTREL. Your servant, madam!

  WITTIPOL whispers with MANLY.

WITTIPOL.   How now? Friend? Offended
  That I have found your haunt here?

MANLY.   No, but wondering
  At your strange-fashioned venture hither.

WITTIPOL.   It is
  To show you what they are you so pursue.

MANLY. I think 'twill prove a medicine against marriage   5
  To know their manners.

WITTIPOL.   Stay, and profit then.

MERECRAFT. The lady, madam, whose prince has brought her
    here
  To be instructed.

  He presents MISTRESS FITZDOTTREL.

WITTIPOL.   Please you sit with us, lady.

MERECRAFT. That's lady-president.

FITZDOTTREL.   A goodly woman!
  I cannot see the ring though.

MERECRAFT.   Sir, she has it.   10

TAILBUSH. But, madam, these are very feeble reasons!

WITTIPOL. So I urged, madam, that the new complexion
　　Now to come forth in name o' your ladyship's fucus
　　Had no ingredient –

TAILBUSH.   But I durst eat, I assure you.

WITTIPOL. So do they in Spain.

TAILBUSH.   Sweet madam, be so liberal   15
　　To give us some o' your Spanish fucuses!

WITTIPOL. They are infinite, madam.

TAILBUSH.   So I hear.

WITTIPOL.   They have
　　Water of gourds, of radish, the white beans,
　　Flowers of glass, of thistles, rosmarine,
　　Raw honey, mustard-seed, and bread dough-baked,   20
　　The crumbs o' bread, goat's milk, and whites of eggs,
　　Camphor, and lily roots, the fat of swans,
　　Marrow of veal, white pigeons, and pine-kernels,
　　The seeds of nettles, purslane, and hare's gall,
　　Lemons thin-skinned –

EITHERSIDE.   How her ladyship has studied   25
　　All excellent things!

WITTIPOL.   But ordinary, madam.
　　No, the true rarities are the alvagada,
　　And argentata of Queen Isabella!

TAILBUSH. Ay, what are their ingredients, gentle madam?

WITTIPOL. Your *allum scagliola*, or *pol di pedra*;   30
　　And *zuccarino*; turpentine of Abezzo,
　　Washed in nine waters; *soda di levante*,
　　Or your fern ashes; *benjamin di gotta*;
　　Grasso di serpe; *porcelletto marino*;
　　Oils of *lentisco*; *zucche*; *mugia* – make   35

The admirable varnish for the face,
Gives the right lustre; but two drops rubbed on
With a piece of scarlet makes a lady of sixty
Look at sixteen. But, above all, the water
Of the white hen, of the Lady Estifania's!   40

TAILBUSH. O, ay, that same, good madam, I have heard of:
How is it done?

WITTIPOL.   Madam, you take your hen,
Plume it, and skin it, cleanse it o' the innards:
Then chop it, bones and all: add to four ounces
Of *carmuacins*, *pipitas*, soap of Cyprus,   45
Make the decoction, strain it. Then distil it,
And keep it in your galley-pot well gliddered.
Three drops preserves from wrinkles, warts, spots, moles,
Blemish, or sun-burnings, and keeps the skin
In decimo sexto, ever bright and smooth,   50
As any looking-glass; and indeed, is called
The virgin's milk for the face, *oglio reale*;
A ceruse, neither cold or heat will hurt;
And mixed with oil of myrrh, and the red gillyflower
Called *caraputia*, and flowers of *rovistico*,   55
Makes the best *muta*, or dye of the whole world.

TAILBUSH. Dear madam, will you let us be familiar?

WITTIPOL. Your ladyship's servant.

MERECRAFT.   How do you like her?

FITZDOTTREL.   Admirable!
But yet, I cannot see the ring.

PUG.   Sir.

MERECRAFT [*aside*].   I must
Deliver it or mar all. This fool's so jealous.   60
Madam –

He is jealous about his ring, and MERECRAFT *delivers it.*
[MERECRAFT *whispers to* WILLIPOL.]

Sir, wear this ring, and pray you take knowledge
'Twas sent you by his wife. And give her thanks.
[*To* PUG.] Do not you dwindle, sir, bear up.

PUG.   I thank you, sir.

TAILBUSH. But for the manner of Spain! Sweet madam, let us
Be bold now we are in: are all the ladies   65
There i' the fashion?

WITTIPOL.   None but grandees, madam,
O' the clasped train, which may be worn at length, too,
Or thus, upon my arm.

TAILBUSH.   And do they wear
Cioppinos all?

WITTIPOL.   If they be dressed in *punto*, madam.   69

EITHERSIDE. Gilt as those are? Madam?

WITTIPOL.   Of goldsmith's work, madam,
And set with diamonds: and their Spanish pumps
Of perfumed leather.

TAILBUSH.   I should think it hard
To go in 'em, madam.

WITTIPOL.   At the first, it is madam.

TAILBUSH. Do you never fall in 'em?

WITTIPOL.   Never.

EITHERSIDE.   I swear, I should
Six times an hour.

TAILBUSH.   But you have men at hand still   75
To help you, if you fall?

WITTIPOL.   Only one, madam,
The guarda-duennas, such a little old man
As this.

[*Points to* TRAINS.]

EITHERSIDE. Alas! he can do nothing! This!

WITTIPOL. I'll tell you, madam, I saw i'the Court of Spain once,   80
    A lady fall i'the King's sight, along.
    And there she lay, flat spread as an umbrella,
    Her hoop here cracked; no man durst reach a hand
    To help her, till the guarda-duennas came,
    Who is the person only'allowed to touch
    A lady there: and he but by his finger.   85

EITHERSIDE. Ha' they no servants, madam, there? Nor friends?

WITTIPOL. An escudero or so, madam, that waits
    Upon 'em in another coach at distance,
    And when they walk, or dance, holds by a handkercher,
    Never presumes to touch 'em.

EITHERSIDE.   This's scurvy!   90
    And a forced gravity! I do not like it.
    I like our own much better.

TAILBUSH.   'Tis more French,
    And courtly ours.

EITHERSIDE.   And tastes more liberty.
    We may have our dozen of visitors, at once,
    Make love to'us.

TAILBUSH.   And before our husbands!

EITHERSIDE.   Husband?   95
    As I am honest, Tailbush, I do think
    If nobody should love me but my poor husband,
    I should e'en hang myself.

TAILBUSH.   Fortune forbid, wench,
    So fair a neck should have so foul a necklace.

EITHERSIDE. 'Tis true, as I am handsome!

WITTIPOL.   I received, lady,   100
    A token from you, which I would not be
    Rude to refuse, being your first remembrance.

FITZDOTTREL. O, I am satisfied now!

MERECRAFT.   Do you see it, sir?

WITTIPOL. But since you come to know me nearer, lady,
  I'll beg the honour you will wear it for me,   105
  It must be so.

  WITTIPOL *gives [the ring to]* MISTRESS FITZDOTTREL.

FRANCES.   Sure I have heard this tongue.

  MERECRAFT *murmurs.*

  What do you mean, sir?

WITTIPOL.   Would you ha' me mercenary?
  We'll recompense it anon, in somewhat else.

  [*Exeunt* MERECRAFT *and* TRAINS.]

FITZDOTTREL [*he is satisfied now he sees it*].
  I do not love to be gulled, though in a toy.
  Wife, do you hear? you're come into the school, wife,   110
  Where you may learn, I do perceive it, anything!
  How to be fine, or fair, or great, or proud,
  Or what you will indeed, wife; here 'tis taught.
  And I am glad on 't, that you may not say
  Another day, when honours come upon you,   115
  You wanted means.

  He upbraids her, with his Bill of costs.

                I ha' done my parts: been
  Today at fifty pound charge, first, for a ring
  To get you entered. Then left my new play
  To wait upon you here, to see't confirmed.
  That I may say both to mine own eyes, and ears –   120
  Senses, you are my witness – she'hath enjoyed
  All helps that could be had for love, or money –

FRANCES. To make a fool of her.

FITZDOTTREL.   Wife, that's your malice,
  The wickedness o'your nature to interpret
  Your husband's kindness thus. But I'll not leave   125

Still to do good for your depraved affections:
Intend it. Bend this stubborn will; be great.

TAILBUSH. Good madam, whom do they use in messages?

WITTIPOL. They commonly use their slaves, madam.

TAILBUSH.   And does your ladyship
Think that so good, madam.

WITTIPOL.   No indeed, madam; I   130
Therein prefer the fashion of England far,
Of your young delicate page, or discreet usher.

FITZDOTTREL. And I go with your ladyship in opinion
Directly for your gentleman-usher;
There's not a finer officer goes on ground.   135

WITTIPOL. If he be made and broken to his place, once.

FITZDOTTREL. Nay, so I presuppose him.

WITTIPOL.   And they are fitter
Managers too, sir, but I would have 'em called
Our escuderos.

FITZDOTTREL. Good.

WITTIPOL.   Say I should send
To your ladyship who, I presume, has gathered   140
All the dear secrets to know how to make
Pastillos of the Duchess of Braganza,
Coquettas, almojavanas, mantecadas,
Alcoreas, mustaccioli; or say it were
The *peladore* of Isabella, or balls   145
Against the itch, or *aqua nanfa,* or oil
Of jessamine for gloves of the Marquess Muja;
Or for the head, and hair: why these are offices –

FITZDOTTREL. Fit for a gentleman, not a slave.

WITTIPOL.   They only
Might ask for your *piveti,* Spanish coal,   150
To burn and sweeten a room; but the arcana

Of ladies' cabinets –

FITZDOTTREL.   Should be elsewhere trusted.
You're much about the truth.

He enters himself with the Ladies.

                              Sweet honoured ladies,
Let me fall in wi' you. I ha' my female wit,
As well as my male. And I do know what suits   155
A lady of spirit, or a woman of fashion!

WITTIPOL. And you would have your wife such.

FITZDOTTREL.   Yes, madam, airy,
Light; not to plain dishonesty, I mean,
But somewhat o' this side.

WITTIPOL.   I take you, sir.
He'has reason, ladies. I'll not give this rush   160
For any lady that cannot be honest
Within a thread.

TAILBUSH.   Yes, madam, and yet venture
As far for th'other, in her fame –

WITTIPOL.   As can be;
Coach it to Pimlico; dance the saraband;
Hear and talk bawdy; laugh as loud, as a larum;   165
Squeak, spring, do anything.

EITHERSIDE.   In young company, madam.

TAILBUSH. Or afore gallants. If they be brave, or lords,
A woman is engaged.

FITZDOTTREL.   I say so, ladies,
It is civility to deny us nothing.

The DEVIL *admires him.*

PUG [*aside*]. You talk of a university! Why, Hell is   170
A grammar school to this!

EITHERSIDE.   But then,
She must not lose a look on stuffs, or cloth, madam.

TAILBUSH. Nor no coarse fellow.

WITTIPOL.   She must be guided, madam,
  By the clothes he wears, and company he is in;
  Whom to salute, how far –

FITZDOTTREL.   I ha' told her this.   175
  And how that bawdry too, upo' the point,
  Is in itself as civil a discourse –

WITTIPOL. As any other affair of flesh, whatever.

FITZDOTTREL. But she will ne'er be capable, she is not
  So much as coming, madam; I know not how,   180
  She loses all her opportunities
  With hoping to be forced. I've entertained
  A gentleman, a younger brother, here,

  He shows his PUG.

  Whom I would fain breed up her escudero
  Against some expectations that I have,   185
  And she'll not countenance him.

WITTIPOL.   What's his name?

FITZDOTTREL. Devil, o' Derbyshire.

EITHERSIDE.   Bless us from him!

TAILBUSH.   Devil?
  Call him De-vile, sweet madam.

FRANCES.   What you please, ladies.

TAILBUSH. De-vile's a prettier name!

EITHERSIDE.   And sounds, methinks,
  As it came in with the Conqueror –

MANLY [*aside*].   Over smocks!   190
  What things they are! That nature should be at leisure
  Ever to make 'em! My wooing is at an end.

  MANLY *goes out with indignation.*

WITTIPOL. What can he do?

EITHERSIDE.   Let's hear him.

TAILBUSH.   Can he manage?

FITZDOTTREL. Please you to try him, ladies. Stand forth, Devil.

PUG [*aside*]. Was all this but the preface to my torment?   195

FITZDOTTREL. Come, let their ladyships see your honours.

    [PUG *bows*.]

EITHERSIDE.   O,
He makes a wicked leg.

TAILBUSH.   As ever I saw!

WITTIPOL. Fit for a Devil.

TAILBUSH.   Good madam, call him De-vile.

They begin their catechism.

WITTIPOL. De-vile, what property is there most required
I'your conceit now in the escudero?   200

FITZDOTTREL. Why do you not speak?

PUG.   A settled discreet pace, madam.

WITTIPOL. I think a barren head, sir, mountain-like,
To be exposed to the cruelty of weathers –

FITZDOTTREL. Ay, for his valley is beneath the waste, madam,
And to be fruitful there, it is sufficient.   205
Dullness upon you! Could not you hit this?

He strikes him.

PUG. Good sir –

WITTIPOL.   He then had had no barren head.
You daw him too much, in troth, sir.

FITZDOTTREL.   I must walk
With the French stick, like an old verger, for you.

The DEVIL *prays.*

PUG. O chief, call me to Hell again, and free me.   210

FITZDOTTREL. Do you murmur now?

PUG.   Not I, sir.

WITTIPOL.   What do you take,
    Master De-vile, the height of your employment
    In the true perfect escudero?

FITZDOTTREL.   When?
    What do you answer?

PUG.   To be able, madam,
    First to enquire, then report the working   215
    Of any lady's physic, in sweet phrase.

WITTIPOL. Yes, that's an act of elegance and importance.
    But what above?

FITZDOTTREL.   O, that I had a goad for him.

PUG. To find out a good corn-cutter.

TAILBUSH.   Out on him!

EITHERSIDE. Most barbarous!

FITZDOTTREL.   Why did you do this, now?   220
    Of purpose to discredit me? You damned Devil.

PUG [aside]. Sure if I be not yet, I shall be. All
    My days in Hell were holy-days to this!

TAILBUSH. 'Tis labour lost, madam!

EITHERSIDE.   He's a dull fellow
    Of no capacity!

TAILBUSH.   Of no discourse!   225
    O, if my Ambler had been here!

EITHERSIDE.   Ay, madam;
    You talk of a man, where is there such another?

WITTIPOL. Master De-vile, put case one of my ladies here
    Had a fine brach, and would employ you forth

To treat 'bout a convenient match for her.   230
What would you observe?

PUG.   The colour, and the size, madam.

WITTIPOL. And nothing else?

FITZDOTTREL.   The moon, you calf, the moon!

WITTIPOL. Ay, and the sign.

TAILBUSH.   Yes, and receipts for proneness.

WITTIPOL. Then when the puppies came, what would you do?

PUG. Get their nativities cast!

WITTIPOL.   This's well. What more?   235

PUG. Consult the almanack-man which would be least?
Which cleanliest?

WITTIPOL.   And which silentest? This's well, madam!
And while she were with puppy?

PUG.   Walk her out,
And air her every morning!

WITTIPOL.   Very good!
And be industrious to kill her fleas?   240

PUG. Yes!

WITTIPOL. He will make a pretty proficient.

PUG [*aside*].   Who,
Coming from Hell, could look for such catechising?
The Devil is an Ass. I do acknowledge it.

  FITZDOTTREL *admires* WITTIPOL.

FITZDOTTREL. The top of woman! All her sex in abstract!
I love her to each syllable falls from her.   245

TAILBUSH. Good madam, give me leave to go aside with him!
And try him a litle!

WITTIPOL.   Do, and I'll withdraw, madam,

With this fair lady: read to her, the while.

TAILBUSH. Come, sir.

The DEVIL *prays again.*

PUG.   Dear chief, relieve me, or I perish.

WITTIPOL. Lady, we'll follow.

[*Exeunt* TAILBUSH, PUG, *and* EITHERSIDE.]

                    You are not jealous, sir?   250

FITZDOTTREL. O, madam! You shall see. Stay wife, behold,
  I give her up here absolutely to you,
  She is your own. Do with her what you will!

He gives his wife to him, taking him to be a lady.

  Melt, cast, and form her as you shall think good!   255
  Set any stamp on! I'll receive her from you
  As a new thing, by your own standard!

WITTIPOL.   Well, sir!

[*Exeunt* MISTRESS FITZDOTTREL *and* WITTIPOL.]

Act IV, Scene v

MERECRAFT. But what ha' you done i'your dependance, since?

FITZDOTTREL. O, it goes on. I met your cousin, the Master –

MERECRAFT. You did not acquaint him, sir?

FITZDOTTREL.   Faith, but I did, sir.
  And upon better thought not without reason!
  He being chief officer might ha' ta'en it ill, else,   5
  As a contempt against his place, and that
  In time, sir, ha' drawn on another dependance.
  No, I did find him in good terms, and ready

To do me any service.

MERECRAFT.   So he said, to you!
But sir, you do not know him.

FITZDOTTREL.   Why, I presumed   10
Because this business of my wife's required me
I could not ha' done better: and he told
Me that he would go presently to your counsel,
A knight, here, i' the lane –

MERECRAFT.   Yes, Justice Eitherside.

FITZDOTTREL. And get the feoffment drawn, with a letter of
          attorney   15
For livery and seisin!

MERECRAFT.   That I know's the course.
But sir, you mean not to make him feoffee?

FITZDOTTREL. Nay, that I'll pause on!

[*Enter* PITFALL.]

MERECRAFT.   How now, little Pitfall!

PITFALL. Your cousin Master Everill would come in
But he would know if Master Manly were here.   20

MERECRAFT. No, tell him; if he were, I ha' made his peace!

[*Exit* PITFALL.] MERECRAFT *whispers against him.*

He's one, sir, has no state, and a man knows not
How such a trust may tempt him.

FITZDOTTREL.   I conceive you.

[*Enter* EVERILL *and* PLUTARCHUS.]

EVERILL. Sir, this same deed is done here.

MERECRAFT.   Pretty Plutarchus!
Art thou come with it? And has Sir Paul viewed it?   25

PLUTARCHUS. His hand is to the draft.

MERECRAFT.   Will you step in, sir

And read it?

FITZDOTTREL. Yes.

EVERILL.   I pray you a word wi' you.

EVERILL *whispers against* MERECRAFT.

Sir Paul Eitherside willed me gi' you caution
Whom you did make feoffee: for 'tis the trust
O' your whole state: and though my cousin here   30
Be a worthy gentleman, yet his valour has
At the tall board been questioned; and we hold
Any man so impeached, of doubtful honesty!
I will not justify this, but give it you
To make your profit of it: if you utter it,   35
I can forswear it!

FITZDOTTREL.   I believe you, and thank you, sir.

[*Exeunt.*]

Act IV, Scene vi

[*Enter*] WITTIPOL, MISTRESS FITZDOTTREL, *and* MANLY.

WITTIPOL. Be not afraid, sweet lady: you're trusted
To love, not violence here. I am no ravisher,
But one whom you, by your fair trust again,
May of a servant make a most true friend.

FRANCES. And such a one I need, but not this way: 5
Sir, I confess me to you, the mere manner
Of your attempting me this morning took me,
And I did hold my' invention, and my manners
Were both engaged to give it a requital;
But not unto your ends: my hope was then –   10
Though interrupted, ere it could be uttered –

That whom I found the master of such language,
That brain and spirit, for such an enterprise
Could not but, if those succours were demanded
To a right use, employ them virtuously!   15
And make that profit of his noble parts,
Which they would yield. Sir, you have now the ground
To exercise them in: I am a woman
That cannot speak more wretchedness of myself
Than you can read; matched to a mass of folly,   20
That every day makes haste to his own ruin;
The wealthy portion that I brought him, spent;
And, through my friends' neglect, no jointure made me.
My fortunes standing in this precipice,
'Tis counsel that I want, and honest aids: 25
And in this name I need you for a friend!
Never in any other; for his ill
Must not make me, sir, worse.

MANLY, *concealed this while, shows himself.*

MANLY.   O friend! Forsake not
    The brave occasion virtue offers you
    To keep you innocent: I have feared for both;   30
    And watched you, to prevent the ill I feared.
    But since the weaker side hath so assured me
    Let not the stronger fall by his own vice,
    Or be the less a friend, 'cause virtue needs him.

WITTIPOL. Virtue shall never ask my succours twice;   35
    Most friend, most man, your counsels are commands:
    Lady, I can love goodness in you more
    Than I did beauty; and do here entitle
    Your virtue to the power, upon a life
    You shall engage in any fruitful service,   40
    Even to forfeit.

[*Enter* MERECRAFT.]

MERECRAFT.   Madam.

[*Exit* MISTRESS FITZDOTTREL.] MERECRAFT *takes*

WITTIPOL *aside, and moves a project for himself.*

                Do you hear, sir,
We have another leg strained for this Dottrel.
He'has a quarrel to carry, and has caused
A deed of feoffment of his whole estate
To be drawn yonder. He'has't within: and you   45
Only he means to make the feoffee. He's fallen
So desperately enamoured on you, and talks
Most like a madman: you did never hear
A frantic so in love with his own favour!
Now you do know 'tis of no validity   50
In your name, as you stand; therefore advise him
To put in me. He's come here. You shall share sir.

Act IV, Scene vii

[*Enter*] FITZDOTTREL, EVERILL, [*and*] PLUTARCHUS.

FITZDOTTREL. Madam, I have a suit to you, and aforehand
   I do bespeak you; you must not deny me,
   I will be granted.

WITTIPOL.   Sir, I must know it though.

FITZDOTTREL. No, lady, you must not know it: yet you must too,
   For the trust of it, and the fame indeed,   5
   Which else were lost me. I would use your name
   But in a feoffment: make my whole estate
   Over unto you: a trifle, a thing of nothing,
   Some eighteen hundred.

WITTIPOL.   Alas! I understand not
   Those things, sir. I am a woman, and most loth   10
   To embark myself –

FITZDOTTREL.   You will not slight me, madam?

WITTIPOL. Nor you'll not quarrel me?

FITZDOTTREL.   No, sweet madam, I have
  Already a dependance, for which cause
  I do this: let me put you in, dear madam,
  I may be fairly killed.

WITTIPOL.   You have your friends, sir,   15
  About you here for choice.

EVERILL.   She tells you right, sir.

  He hopes to be the man.

FITZDOTTREL. Death, if she do, what do I care for that?
  Say I would have her tell me wrong.

WITTIPOL.   Why, sir,
  If for the trust, you'll let me have the honour
  To name you one.

FITZDOTTREL.   Nay, you do me the honour, madam.   20
  Who is't?

WITTIPOL. This gentleman.

  She designs MANLY.

FITZDOTTREL.   O no, sweet madam,
  He's friend to him with whom I ha' the dependance.

WITTIPOL. Who might he be?

FITZDOTTREL.   One Wittipol: do you know him?

WITTIPOL. Alas, sir, he, a toy: this gentleman
  A friend to him? No more than I am, sir!   25

FITZDOTTREL. But will your ladyship undertake that, madam?

WITTIPOL. Yes, and what else for him you will engage me.

FITZDOTTREL. What is his name?

WITTIPOL.   His name is Eustace Manly.

FITZDOTTREL. Whence does he write himself?

WITTIPOL.   Of Middlesex,
  Esquire.

FITZDOTTREL. Say nothing, madam. Clerk, come hither,   30
    Write Eustace Manly, squire o' Middlesex.

MERECRAFT. What ha' you done, sir?

WITTIPOL.   Named a gentleman
    That I'll be answerable for to you, sir.
    Had I named you, it might ha' been suspected:
    This way 'tis safe.

FITZDOTTREL.   Come gentlemen, your hands   35
    For witness.

MANLY.   What is this?

EVERILL [*applauds it*].   You ha' made election
    Of a most worthy gentleman!

MANLY.   Would one
    Of worth had spoke it: whence it comes, it is
    Rather a shame to me than a praise.

EVERILL. Sir, I will give you any satisfaction.   40

MANLY. Be silent then: 'falsehood commends not truth.'

PLUTARCHUS. You do deliver this, sir, as your deed.
    To the'use of Master Manly?

FITZDOTTREL.   Yes: and sir –
    When did you see young Wittipol? I am ready
    For process now; sir, this is publication.   45
    He shall hear from me; he would needs be courting
    My wife, sir.

MANLY.   Yes: so witnesseth his cloak there.

    FITZDOTTREL *is suspicious of* MANLY *still.*

FITZDOTTREL. Nay good sir – madam, you did undertake –

WITTIPOL. What?

FITZDOTTREL.   That he was not Wittipol's friend.

WITTIPOL.   I hear
    Sir, no confession of it.

FITZDOTTREL.   O she knows not;   50
  Now I remember, madam! This young Wittipol
  Would ha' debauched my wife, and made me cuckold
  Through a casement. He did fly her home
  To mine own window; but I think I soused him,
  And ravished her away, out of his pounces.   55
  I ha' sworn to ha'him by the ears: I fear
  The toy will'not do me right.

WITTIPOL.   No? That were pity!
  What right do you ask, sir? Here he is will do't you!

  WITTIPOL *discovers himself.*

FITZDOTTREL. Ha? Wittipol?

WITTIPOL.   Ay, sir, no more lady now,
  Nor Spaniard!

MANLY.   No indeed, 'tis Wittipol.   60

FITZDOTTREL. Am I the thing I feared?

WITTIPOL.   A cuckold? No sir,
  But you were late in possibility,
  I'll tell you so much.

MANLY.   But your wife's too virtuous!

WITTIPOL. We'll see her, sir, at home, and leave you here
  To be made Duke o' Shoreditch with a project.   65

FITZDOTTREL. Thieves, ravishers!

WITTIPOL.   Cry but another note, sir,
  I'll mar the tune o' your pipe.

FITZDOTTREL [*he would have his deed again*].
        Gi' me my deed, then.

WITTIPOL. Neither: that shall be kept for your wife's good,
  Who will know better how to use it.

FITZDOTTREL.   Ha!
  To feast you with my land?

WITTIPOL.   Sir, be you quiet,   70
  Or I shall gag you ere I go; consult
  Your Master of Dependances how to make this
  A second business, you have time, sir.

  WITTIPOL baffles him, and goes out.

FITZDOTTREL.   O!
  What will the ghost of my wise grandfather,
  My learned father, with my worshipful mother   75
  Think of me now, that left me in this world
  In state to be their heir? That am become
  A cuckold, and an ass, and my wife's ward;
  Likely to lose my land, ha' my throat cut,
  All, by her practice!

MERECRAFT.   Sir, we are all abused!   80

FITZDOTTREL. And be so still! Who hinders you? I pray you,
  Let me alone, I would enjoy myself,
  And be the Duke o' Drowned-land, you ha' made me.

MERECRAFT. Sir, we must play an after-game o' this.

FITZDOTTREL. But I am not in case to be a gamester: 85
  I tell you once again –

MERECRAFT.   You must be ruled
  And take some counsel.

FITZDOTTREL.   Sir, I do hate counsel,
  As I do hate my wife, my wicked wife!

MERECRAFT. But we may think how to recover all,
  If you will act.

FITZDOTTREL. I will not think, nor act,   90
  Nor yet recover; do not talk to me!
  I'll run out o' my wits rather than hear;
  I will be what I am, Fabian Fitzdottrel,
  Though all the world say nay to't. [*Exit.*]

MERECRAFT. Let's follow him. [*Exeunt.*]

Act V, Scene i

[*Enter*] AMBLER [*and*] PITFALL.

AMBLER. But has my lady missed me?

PITFALL.   Beyond telling!
　Here has been that infinity of strangers!
　And then she would ha' had you to ha' sampled you
　With one within that they are now a-teaching,
　And does pretend to your rank.

AMBLER.   Good fellow Pitfall,   5
　Tell Master Merecraft I entreat a word with him.

　PITFALL *goes out*.

　This most unlucky accident will go near
　To be the loss o'my place, I am in doubt!

[*Enter* MERECRAFT.]

MERECRAFT. With me? What say you Master Ambler?

AMBLER.   Sir,
　I would beseech your worship stand between   10
　Me and my lady's displeasure for my absence.

MERECRAFT. O, is that all? I warrant you.

AMBLER.   I would tell you, sir,
　But how it happened.

MERECRAFT.   Brief, good Master Ambler,
　Put yourself to your rack, for I have task
　Of more importance.

　MERECRAFT *seems full of business*.

AMBLER.   Sir, you'll laugh at me!   15

But – so is truth – a very friend of mine,
Finding by conference with me, that I lived
Too chaste for my complexion – and indeed
Too honest for my place, sir – did advise me
If I did love myself – as that I do   20
I must confess –

MERECRAFT.   Spare your parenthesis.

AMBLER. To gi' my body a little evacuation –

MERECRAFT. Well, and you went to a whore?

AMBLER.   No, sir. I durst not –
For fear it might arrive at somebody's ear
It should not – trust myself to a common house,   25

AMBLER tells this with extraordinary speed.

But got the gentlewoman to go with me,
And carry her bedding to a conduit-head,
Hard by the place toward Tyburn, which they call
My Lord Mayor's Banqueting House. Now, sir, this morning
Was execution; and I ne'er dreamed on't   30
Till I heard the noise o' the people and the horses;
And neither I nor the poor gentlewoman
Durst stir till all was done and past: so that
I'the interim we fell asleep again.

He flags.

MERECRAFT. Nay, if you fall from your gallop I am gone, sir. 35

AMBLER. But when I waked, to put on my clothes, a suit
I made new for the action, it was gone,
And all my money, with my purse, my seals,
My hard-wax, and my table-books, my studies,
And a fine new device I had to carry   40
My pen and ink, my civet, and my toothpicks,
All under one. But that which grieved me was
The gentlewoman's shoes, with a pair of roses
And garters I had given her for the business,
So as that made us stay till it was dark;   45

For I was fain to lend her mine, and walk
In a rug by her, barefoot to Saint Giles's.

MERECRAFT. A kind of Irish penance! Is this all, sir?

AMBLER. To satisfy my lady.

MERECRAFT.   I will promise you, sir.

AMBLER. I ha' told the true disaster.

MERECRAFT.   I cannot stay wi' you,   50
Sir, to condole, but gratulate your return.

[*Exit.*]

AMBLER. An honest gentleman, but he's never at leisure
To be himself: he has such tides of business.

[*Exit.*]

Act V, Scene ii

[*Enter*] PUG.

PUG. O call me home again, dear chief, and put me
To yoking foxes, milking of he-goats,
Pounding of water in a mortar, laving
The sea dry with a nutshell, gathering all
The leaves are fallen this autumn, drawing farts   5
Out of dead bodies, making ropes of sand,
Catching the winds together in a net,
Must'ring of ants, and numbering atoms; all
That hell and you thought exquisite torments, rather
Than stay me here a thought more: I would sooner   10
Keep fleas within a circle, and be accountant
A thousand year which of 'em and how far
Out-leaped the other, than endure a minute
Such as I have within. There is no hell

To a lady of fashion. All your tortures there   15
Are pastimes to it. 'Twould be a refreshing
For me to be i'the fire again, from hence.

AMBLER *comes in and surveys him.*

AMBLER. This is my suit, and those the shoes and roses!

PUG. They've such impertinent vexations,
  A general council o' devils could not hit –   20

PUG *perceives it, and starts.*

Ha! This is he I took asleep with his wench,
And borrowed his clothes. What might I do to balk him?

AMBLER. Do you hear, sir?

PUG [*aside*].   Answer him, but not to th'purpose.

AMBLER. What is your name, I pray you, sir?

PUG [*he answers quite from the purpose*].   Is't so late, sir?

AMBLER. I ask not o'the time, but of your name, sir.   25

PUG. I thank you, sir. Yes it does hold, sir, certain.

AMBLER. Hold, sir? What holds? I must both hold, and talk to you
  About these clothes.

PUG.   A very pretty lace!
  But the tailor cozened me.

AMBLER.   No, I am cozened
  By you! Robbed!

PUG.   Why when you please sir, I am   30
  For threepenny gleek, your man.

AMBLER.   Pox o'your gleek,
  And threepence! Give me an answer.

PUG.   Sir,
  My master is the best at it.

AMBLER.   Your master!
  Who is your master?

PUG.   Let it be Friday night.   34

AMBLER. What should be then?

PUG.   Your best song's 'Tom o' Bedlam'.

AMBLER. I think you are he. Does he mock me, trow, from purpose?
    Or do not I speak to him what I mean?
    Good sir, your name.

PUG.   Only a couple o' cocks sir,
    If we can get a widgeon, 'tis in season.

AMBLER. He hopes to make one o'these Sciptics o' me –   40

    (*For Sceptics.*)

    I think I name 'em right – and does not fly me.
    I wonder at that! 'Tis a strange confidence!
    I'll prove another way to draw his answer.

    [*Exit.*]

Act V, Scene iii

[*Enter*] MERECRAFT, FITZDOTTREL, [*and*] EVERILL.

MERECRAFT. It is the easiest thing, sir, to be done.
    As plain as fizzling: roll but wi' your eyes,
    And foam at th'mouth. A little castle-soap
    Will do't, to rub your lips: and then a nutshell,
    With tow and touchwood in it to spit fire.   5
    Did you ne'er read, sir, little Darrel's tricks,
    With the boy o'Burton, and the seven in Lancashire,
    Sommers at Nottingham? All these do teach it.
    And we'll give out, sir, that your wife has bewitched you –

EVERILL. And practised with those two, as sorcerers.   10

    They repair their old plot.

MERECRAFT. And ga' you potions by which means you were
Not *compos mentis* when you made your feoffment.
There's no recovery o' your state but this;
This, sir, will sting.

EVERILL.   And move in a court of equity.

MERECRAFT. For it is more than manifest that this was   15
A plot o' your wife's to get your land.

FITZDOTTREL.   I think it.

EVERILL. Sir, it appears.

MERECRAFT.   Nay, and my cousin has known
These gallants in these shapes.

EVERILL.   To'have done strange things, sir.
One as the lady, the other as the squire.   19

MERECRAFT. How a man's honesty may be fooled! I thought him
A very lady.

FITZDOTTREL. So did I: renounce me else.

MERECRAFT. But this way, sir, you'll be revenged at height.

EVERILL. Upon 'em all.

MERECRAFT.   Yes, faith, and since your wife
Has run the way of woman thus, e'en give her –

FITZDOTTREL. Lost, by this hand, to me: dead to all joys   25
Of her dear Dottrel! I shall never pity her
That could pity herself.

MERECRAFT.   Princely resolved sir,
And like yourself still, *in potentia.*

Act V, Scene iv

[*Enter*] GILTHEAD, PLUTARCHUS, SLEDGE, [*and*]
    SERGEANTS.

MERECRAFT. Gilthead, what news?

   FITZDOTTREL *asks for his money*.

FITZDOTTREL.   O sir, my hundred pieces:
    Let me ha' them yet.

GILTHEAD.   Yes, sir. Officers,
    Arrest him.

FITZDOTTREL. Me?

SERGEANT.   I arrest you.

SLEDGE.   Keep the peace,
    I charge you, gentlemen.

FITZDOTTREL. Arrest me? Why?

GILTHEAD. For better security, sir. My son Plutarchus   5
    Assures me, you're not worth a groat.

PLUTARCHUS.   Pardon me, father,
    I said his worship had no foot of land left:
    And that I'll justify, for I writ the deed.

FITZDOTTREL. Ha' you these tricks i'the city?

GILTHEAD.   Yes, and more.
    Arrest this gallant too, here, at my suit.   10

   Meaning MERECRAFT.

SLEDGE. Ay, and at mine. He owes me for his lodging
    Two year and a quarter.

MERECRAFT.   Why Master Gilthead, landlord,
    Thou art not mad, though thou'art constable,
    Puffed up with th'pride of the place? Do you hear, sirs?
    Have I deserved this from you two for all   15
    My pains at Court to get you each a patent.

GILTHEAD. For what?

The project of forks.

MERECRAFT.   Upo' my project o'the forks.

SLEDGE. Forks? What be they?

MERECRAFT.   The laudable use of forks,
  Brought into custom here, as they are in Italy,
  To th'sparing o' napkins. That, that should have made   20
  Your bellows go at the forge, as his at the furnace.
  I ha' procured it, ha' the signet for it.
  Dealt with the linen-drapers, on my private,
  By cause, I feared, they were the likeliest ever
  To stir against, to cross it: for 'twill be   25
  A mighty saver of linen through the kingdom –
  As that is one o' my grounds, and to spare washing –
  Now on you two had I laid all the profits:
  Gilthead to have the making of all those
  Of gold and silver, for the better personages,   30
  And you of those of steel for the common sort.
  And both by patent. I had brought you your seals in.
  But now you have prevented me, and I thank you.

  SLEDGE *is brought about.*

SLEDGE. Sir, I will bail you, at mine own apperil.

  And GILTHEAD *comes.*

MERECRAFT. Nay, choose.

PLUTARCHUS.   Do you so too, good father.   35

GILTHEAD. I like the fashion o' the project well:
  The forks! It may be a lucky one! And is not
  Intricate, as one would say, but fit for
  Plain heads, as ours, to deal in. Do you hear,
  Officers, we discharge you.

  [*Exeunt* SERGEANTS.]

MERECRAFT.   Why this shows   40

A little good nature in you, I confess,
But do not tempt your friends thus. Little Gilthead,
Advise your sire, great Gilthead, from these courses:
And here to trouble a great man in reversion,
For a matter o'fifty on a false alarm,   45
Away, it shows not well. Let him get the pieces
And bring 'em. You'll hear more else.

PLUTARCHUS.   Father.

  [*Exit with* GILTHEAD.]

Act V, Scene v

[*Enter*] AMBLER.

AMBLER. O, Master Sledge, are you here? I ha' been to seek you.
    You are the constable, they say. Here's one
    That I do charge with felony, for the suit
    He wears, sir.

MERECRAFT.   Who? Master Fitzdottrel's man?
    'Ware what you do, Master Ambler.

AMBLER.   Sir, these clothes,   5
    I'll swear, are mine: and the shoes the gentlewoman's
    I told you of: and ha' him afore a Justice
    I will.

PUG.   My master, sir, will pass his word for me.

AMBLER. O, can you speak to purpose now?

    FITZDOTTREL *disclaims him.*

FITZDOTTREL.   Not I.
    If you be such a one, sir, I will leave you   10
    To your godfathers in law. Let twelve men work.

PUG. Do you hear sir; pray, in private.

FITZDOTTREL.   Well, what say you?
  Brief, for I have no time to lose.

PUG.   Truth is sir,
  I am the very Devil, and had leave
  To take this body I am in to serve you;   15
  Which was a cutpurse's, and hanged this morning.
  And it is likewise true I stole this suit
  To clothe me with. But, sir, let me not go
  To prison for it. I have hitherto
  Lost time, done nothing; shown, indeed, no part   20
  O' my devil's nature. Now I will so help
  Your malice 'gainst these parties: so advance
  The business that you have in hand of witchcraft,
  And your possession, as myself were in you;
  Teach you such tricks, to make your belly swell,   25
  And your eyes turn, to foam, to stare, to gnash
  Your teeth together, and to beat yourself,
  Laugh loud, and feign six voices –

FITZDOTTREL.   Out, you rogue!
  You most infernal counterfeit wretch! Avaunt!
  Do you think to gull me with your Aesop's *Fables*?   30
  Here, take him to you, I ha' no part in him.

PUG.   Sir!

FITZDOTTREL. Away, I do disclaim; I will not hear you.

And sends him away [with SLEDGE].

MERECRAFT. What said he to you, sir?

FITZDOTTREL.   Like a lying rascal
  Told me he was the Devil.

MERECRAFT.   How! A good jest!

FITZDOTTREL. And that he would teach me, such fine devil's
      tricks   35
  For our new resolution.

EVERILL.   O'pox on him!
  'Twas excellent wisely done, sir, not to trust him.

MERECRAFT. Why, if he were the Devil, we sha' not need him,
  If you'll be ruled.

  MERECRAFT *gives the instructions to him and the rest.*

                     Go throw yourself on a bed, sir,
  And feign you ill. We'll not be seen wi' you,   40
  Till after that you have a fit, and all
  Confirmed within. [*To* EVERILL.] Keep you with the two ladies
  And persuade them. I'll to Justice Eitherside,
  And possess him with all, Trains shall seek out Engine,
  And they two fill the town with't; every cable   45
  Is to be veered. We must employ out all
  Our emissaries now. Sir, I will send you
  Bladders and bellows. Sir, be confident,
  'Tis no hard thing t'outdo the Devil in:
  A boy o' thirteen year old made him an ass   50
  But t'other day.

FITZDOTTREL.   Well, I'll begin to practise,
  And scape the imputation of being cuckold,
  By mine own act.

MERECRAFT.   You're right.

  [*Exit* FITZDOTTREL.]

EVERILL.   Come, you ha' put
  Yourself to a simple coil here, and your friends,
  By dealing with new agents, in new plots.   55

MERECRAFT. No more o' that, sweet cousin.

EVERILL.   What had you
  To do with this same Wittipol, for a lady?

MERECRAFT. Question not that: 'tis done.

EVERILL.   You had some strain
  'Bove E-la?

MERECRAFT. I had indeed.

EVERILL.   And now you crack for't.   59

MERECRAFT. Do not upbraid me.

EVERILL.   Come, you must be told on't;
    You are so covetous still to embrace
    More than you can, that you lose all.

MERECRAFT.   'Tis right.
    What would you more, than guilty? Now, your succours.

    [*Exeunt.*]

Act V, Scene vi

[*Enter*] SHACKLES [*and*] PUG.

PUG *is brought to Newgate.*

SHACKLES. Here you are lodged, sir; you must send your garnish,
    If you'll be private.

PUG.   There it is, sir, leave me.

    [*Exit* SHACKLES.]

    To Newgate brought? How is the name of Devil
    Discredited in me! What a lost fiend
    Shall I be on return! My chief will roar   5
    In triumph, now that I have been on earth
    A day, and done no noted thing, but brought
    That body back here was hanged out this morning.

Enter INIQUITY *the Vice.*

    Well! Would it once were midnight, that I knew
    My utmost. I think Time be drunk, and sleeps;   10
    He is so still and moves not? I do glory
    Now i'my torment. Neither can I expect it,

I have it with my fact.

INIQUITY.   Child of hell, be thou merry:
    Put a look on as round, boy, and red as a cherry.
    Cast care at thy posterns and firk i'thy fetters,   15
    They are ornaments, baby, have graced thy betters:
    Look upon me and harken. Our chief doth salute thee,
    And lest the cold iron should chance to confute thee,
    He'hath sent thee grant-parole by me to stay longer
    A month here on earth against cold, child, or hunger –   20

PUG. How? Longer here a month?

INIQUITY.   Yes, boy, till the Session,
    That so thou mayest have a triumphal egression.

PUG. In a cart, to be hanged.

INIQUITY.   No, child, in a car,
    The chariot of triumph, which most of them are.
    And in the mean time, to be greasy and bouzy,   25
    And nasty and filthy, and ragged and lousy,
    With damn me, renounce me, and all the fine phrases,
    That bring unto Tyburn the plentiful gazes.

PUG. He is a devil! And may be our chief!
    The great superior devil! For his malice,   30
    Arch-devil! I acknowledge him. He knew
    What I would suffer when he tied me up thus
    In a rogue's body: and he has, I thank him,
    His tyrannous pleasure on me, to confine me
    To the unlucky carcass of a cutpurse,   35
    Wherein I could do nothing.

The great DEVIL *enters, and upbraids him with all his day's work.*

SATAN.   Impudent fiend
    Stop thy lewd mouth. Dost thou not shame and tremble
    To lay thine own dull damned defects upon
    An innocent case there? Why, thou heavy slave!
    The spirit that did possess that flesh before   40
    Put more true life in a finger and a thumb,

Than thou in the whole mass. Yet thou rebell'st
And murmur'st! What one proffer hast thou made,
Wicked enough, this day, that might be called
Worthy thine own, much less the name that sent thee?   45
First, thou didst help thyself into a beating
Promptly, and with't endanger'dst too thy tongue:
A devil, and could not keep a body entire
One day! That, for our credit. And to vindicate it,
Hinder'dst, for aught thou know'st, a deed of darkness: 50
Which was an act of that egregious folly,
As no one to'ard the Devil could ha'thought on.
This for your acting! But for suffering! Why,
Thou hast been cheated on with a false beard,
And a turned cloak. Faith, would your predecessor,   55
The cutpurse, think you, ha'been so? Out upon thee!
The hurt thou'hast done, to let men know their strength,
And that they're able to outdo a devil
Put in a body, will for ever be
A scar upon our name! Whom hast thou dealt with,   60
Woman or man, this day, but have outgone thee
Some way, and most have proved the better fiends?
Yet you would be employed! Yes, Hell shall make you
Provincial o'the cheaters! Or bawd-ledger
For this side o' the town! No doubt you'll render   65
A rare account of things. Bane o' your itch,
And scratching for employment. I'll ha' brimstone
To allay it sure, and fire to singe your nails off.
But that I would not such a damned dishonour
Stick on our state, as that the Devil were hanged,   70
And could not save a body, that he took
From Tyburn, but it must come thither again,
You should e'en ride. But up, away with him!

INIQUITY *takes him on his back.*

INIQUITY. Mount, darling of darkness, my shoulders are broad:
He that carries the fiend is sure of his load.   75
The Devil was wont to carry away the evil;
But now the evil out-carries the Devil. [*Exeunt.*]

Act V, Scene vii

A great noise is heard in Newgate, and [SHACKLES *and*] *the* KEEPERS
come out affrighted.

SHACKLES. O me!

1 KEEPER.   What's this?

2 KEEPER.   A piece of Justice Hall
  Is broken down.

3 KEEPER.   Foh! What a steam of brimstone
  Is here!

4 KEEPER. The prisoner's dead, came in but now!

SHACKLES. Ha? Where?

4 KEEPER.   Look here.

1 KEEPER.   'Slid, I should know his countenance!
  It is Gill Cutpurse, was hanged out this morning!   5

SHACKLES. 'Tis he!

2 KEEPER.   The Devil, sure, has a hand in this!

3 KEEPER. What shall we do?

SHACKLES.   Carry the news of it
  Unto the sheriffs.

1 KEEPER.   And to the Justices.

4 KEEPER. This's strange!

3 KEEPER.   And savours of the Devil strongly!

2 KEEPER. I'ha' the sulphur of hell-coal i'my nose.   10

1 KEEPER. Foh!

SHACKLES.   Carry him in.

1 KEEPER.   Away.

2 KEEPER.   How rank it is!

  [*Exeunt.*]

Act V, Scene viii

[*Enter*] SIR PAUL EITHERSIDE, MERECRAFT, EVERILL,
LADY TAILBUSH, LADY EITHERSIDE, PITFALL, TRAINS,
[*and*] AMBLER. THE JUSTICE *comes out wondering, and the rest
informing him.*

PAUL. This was the notablest conspiracy
    That e'er I heard of.

MERECRAFT.   Sir, they had given him potions
    That did enamour him on the counterfeit lady.

EVERILL. Just to the time o'delivery o'the deed –   4

MERECRAFT. And then the witchcraft 'gan to'appear, for straight
    He fell into his fit.

EVERILL.   Of rage at first, sir,
    Which since has so increased.

TAILBUSH.   Good Sir Paul, see him,
    And punish the impostors.

PAUL.   Therefore I come, madam.

EITHERSIDE. Let Master Eitherside alone, madam.

PAUL.   Do you hear?
    Call in the constable, I will have him by: 10
    He's the King's officer! And some citizens
    Of credit! I'll discharge my conscience clearly.

MERECRAFT. Yes, sir, and send for his wife.

EVERILL.   And the two sorcerers,
    By any means!

    [*Exit a* WAITER.]

TAILBUSH.   I thought one a true lady,
    I should be sworn. So did you, Eitherside!   15

EITHERSIDE. Yes, by that light, would I might ne'er stir else,
    Tailbush.

TAILBUSH. And the other a civil gentleman.

EVERILL.   But, madam,
   You know what I told your ladyship.

TAILBUSH.   I now see it:
   I was providing of a banquet for 'em,
   After I had done instructing o'the fellow   20
   De-vile, the gentleman's man.

MERECRAFT.   Who's found a thief, madam,
   And to have robbed your usher, Master Ambler,
   This morning.

TAILBUSH.   How?

MERECRAFT.   I'll tell you more anon.

   [FITZDOTTREL *on the bed*] *begins his fit.*

FITZDOTTREL. Gi'me some *garlic, garlic, garlic, garlic.*

MERECRAFT. Hark the poor gentleman, how he is tormented!   25

FITZDOTTREL. *My wife is a whore, I'll kiss her no more: and why?*
   Mayst not thou be a cuckold, as well as I?
   Ha, ha, ha, ha, ha, ha, ha, ha etc.

   THE JUSTICE *interprets all.*

PAUL. That is the Devil speaks and laughs in him.

MERECRAFT. Do you think so, sir?

PAUL.   I discharge my conscience.   30

FITZDOTTREL. *And is not the Devil good company? Yes, wis.*

EVERILL. How he changes, sir, his voice!

FITZDOTTREL.   *And a cuckold is,*
   Where e'er he put his head with a wanion
   If his horns be forth, the Devil's companion!
   Look, look, look, else.

MERECRAFT.   How he foams!

EVERILL.   And swells!   35

TAILBUSH. O, me! What's that there rises in his belly!

EITHERSIDE. A strange thing! Hold it down.

TRAINS, PITFALL.   We cannot, madam.

PAUL. 'Tis too apparent this!

> WITTIPOL, *and* MANLY, *and* MISTRESS FITZDOTTREL
> *enter.*

FITZDOTTREL.   *Wittipol, Wittipol.*

WITTIPOL. How now, what play ha' we here?

MANLY.   What fine new matters?

WITTIPOL. The coxcomb, and the coverlet.

MERECRAFT.   O strange impudence!
  That these should come to face their sin!   41

EVERILL.   And outface
  Justice: they are the parties, sir.

PAUL.   Say nothing.

MERECRAFT. Did you mark, sir, upon their coming in,
  How he called Wittipol?

EVERILL.   And never saw 'em.

PAUL. I warrant you did I; let 'em play a while.   45

FITZDOTTREL. *Buzz, buzz, buzz, buzz.*

TAILBUSH.   'Las poor gentleman!
  How he is tortured!

FRANCES.   Fie, Master Fitzdottrel!
  What do you mean to counterfeit thus?

> *His wife goes to him.*

FITZDOTTREL.   *O, O,*
  She comes with a needle, and thrusts it in,
  She pulls out that, and she puts in a pin,   50
  And now, and now, I do not know how, nor where,
  But she pricks me here, and she pricks me there: O, O –

PAUL. Woman, forbear.

WITTIPOL.   What, sir?

PAUL.   A practice foul
  For one so fair.

WITTIPOL.   Hath this then credit with you?

MANLY. Do you believe in't?

PAUL.   Gentlemen, I'll discharge   55
  My conscience. 'Tis a clear conspiracy!
  A dark, and devilish practice! I detest it.

WITTIPOL. The Justice sure will prove the merrier man!

MANLY. This is most strange, sir!

PAUL.   Come not to confront
  Authority with impudence: I tell you,   60
  I do detest it.

  [*Enter* SLEDGE, *and* GILTHEAD.]

             Here comes the King's constable,
  And with him a right worshipful commoner:
  My good friend, Master Gilthead! I am glad
  I can before such witnesses profess
  My conscience and my detestation of it.   65
  Horrible! Most unnatural! Abominable!

  [EVERILL *and* MERECRAFT] *whisper him.*

EVERILL. You do not tumble enough.

MERECRAFT.   Wallow! Gnash!

TAILBUSH. O, how he is vexed!

PAUL.   'Tis too manifest.

EVERILL. Give him more soap to foam with. Now lie still.

  And give him soap to act with.

MERECRAFT. And act a little.

TAILBUSH.   What does he now, sir?

PAUL.   Show   70
    The taking of tobacco, with which the Devil
    Is so delighted.

FITZDOTTREL. *Hum!*

PAUL.   And calls for hum.
    You takers of strong waters and tobacco,
    Mark this.

FITZDOTTREL. *Yellow, yellow, yellow, yellow, etc.*

PAUL. That's starch! The Devil's idol of that colour.   75
    He ratifies it with clapping of his hands.
    The proofs are pregnant.

GILTHEAD.   How the Devil can act!

PAUL. He is the master of players! Master Gilthead,
    And poets, too! You heard him talk in rhyme!
    I had forgot to observe it to you, erewhile!   80

TAILBUSH. See, he spits fire.

PAUL.   O no, he plays at figgum,
    The Devil is the author of wicked figgum.

    SIR PAUL *interprets* Figgum *to be a juggler's game.*

MANLY. Why speak you not unto him?

WITTIPOL.   If I had
    All innocence of man to be endangered,
    And he could save, or ruin it, I'd not breathe   85
    A syllable in request to such a fool
    He makes himself.

FITZDOTTREL. *O, they whisper, whisper, whisper.*
    We shall have more, of devils a score,
    To come to dinner, in me the sinner.

EITHERSIDE. Alas, poor gentleman!

PAUL.   Put 'em asunder.   90

Keep 'em one from the other.

MANLY.   Are you frantic, sir,
Or what grave dotage moves you to take part
With so much villainy? We are not afraid
Either of law or trial; let us be
Examined what our ends were, what the means,   95
To work by; and possibility of those means.
Do not conclude against us ere you hear us.

PAUL. I will not hear you, yet I will conclude
Out of the circumstances.

MANLY.   Will you so, sir?

PAUL. Yes, they are palpable.

MANLY.   Not as your folly.   100

PAUL. I will discharge my conscience, and do all
To the meridian of justice.

GILTHEAD.   You do well, sir.

FITZDOTTREL. *Provide me to eat, three or four dishes o' good meat,*
I'll feast 'em, and their trains, a Justice head and brains
Shall be the first.

PAUL.   The Devil loves not justice,   105
There you may see.

FITZDOTTREL.   *A spare-rib o'my wife,*
And a whore's purtenance! A Gilthead whole.

PAUL. Be not you troubled, sir, the Devil speaks it.

FITZDOTTREL. *Yes, wis, knight, shite, Poule, jowl, owl, foul, troule, boul.*

PAUL. Crambe, another of the Devil's games!   110

MERECRAFT. Speak, sir, some Greek, if you can. Is not the Justice
A solemn gamester?

EVERILL.   Peace.

FITZDOTTREL.   *Oimoi kakadaimōn,*
Kai triskakodaimōn, kai tetrakis, kai pentakis,

Kai dodekakis, kai muriakis.

PAUL.   He curses
  In Greek, I think.

EVERILL.   Your Spanish that I taught you.   115

FITZDOTTREL. *Quebrémos el ojo de burlas.*

EVERILL.   How? Your rest –
  Let's break his neck in jest, the Devil says.

FITZDOTTREL. *Di grátia, Signòr mio se haúete denári fataméne parte.*

MERECRAFT. What, would the Devil borrow money?

FITZDOTTREL.   *Oui,*
  Oui monsieur, un pauvre diable! Diabletin!   120

PAUL. It is the Devil, by his several languages

  Enter [SHACKLES], *the* KEEPER *of Newgate.*

SHACKLES. Where's Sir Paul Eitherside?

PAUL.   Here, what's the matter?

SHACKLES. O! Such an accident fallen out at Newgate, sir:
  A great piece of the prison is rent down!
  The Devil has been there, sir, in the body   125
  Of the young cutpurse was hanged out this morning,
  But in new clothes, sir; every one of us know him.
  These things were found in his pocket.

AMBLER.   Those are mine, sir.

SHACKLES. I think he was committed on your charge, sir,
  For a new felony.

AMBLER.   Yes.

SHACKLES.   He's gone, sir, now,   130
  And left us the dead body. But withal, sir,
  Such an infernal stink and steam behind
  You cannot see St Pulchre's steeple yet;
  They smell't as far as Ware as the wind lies
  By this time, sure.

FITZDOTTREL.   Is this upon your credit, friend?   135

SHACKLES. Sir, you may see, and satisfy yourself.

    FITZDOTTREL *leaves counterfeiting.*

FITZDOTTREL. Nay then, 'tis time to leave off counterfeiting.
    Sir, I am not bewitched, nor have a devil:
    No more than you. I do defy him, I,
    And did abuse you. These two gentlemen   140
    Put me upon it. (I have faith against him.)
    They taught me all my tricks. I will tell truth
    And shame the fiend. See here, sir, are my bellows,
    And my false belly, and my mouse, and all
    That should ha' come forth!

MANLY.   Sir, are not you ashamed   145
    Now of your solemn, serious vanity?

PAUL. I will make honourable amends to truth.

FITZDOTTREL. And so will I. But these are cozeners, still;
    And ha' my land, as plotters with my wife:
    Who, though she be not a witch, is worse – a whore.   150

MANLY. Sir, you belie her. She is chaste, and virtuous,
    And we are honest. I do know no glory
    A man should hope by venting his own follies,
    But you'll still be an ass, in spite of providence.
    Please you go in, sir, and hear truths, then judge 'em: 155
    And make amends for your late rashness; when,
    You shall but hear the pains and care was taken,
    To save this fool from ruin, his Grace of Drowned-land.

FITZDOTTREL. My land is drowned indeed –

PAUL.   Peace.

MANLY.   And how much
    His modest, and too worthy wife hath suffered   160
    By misconstruction from him, you will blush,
    First, for your own belief, more for his actions!
    His land is his: and never, by my friend,

Or by myself, meant to another use
But for her succours, who hath equal right.   165
If any other had worse counsels in't –
I know I speak to those can apprehend me –
Let 'em repent 'em, and be not detected.
It is not manly to take joy, or pride
In human errors. We do all ill things: 170
They do 'em worst that love 'em, and dwell there,
Till the plague comes. The few that have the seeds
Of goodness left will sooner make their way
To a true life by shame, than punishment.

The End.

The Epilogue

Thus the projector here is overthrown.
     But I have now a project of mine own,
If it may pass: that no man would invite
     The poet from us to sup forth tonight,
If the play please. If it displeasant be,
     We do presume that no man will: nor we.

Glossary

Almain leap – high jump in dancing

Alvagada – white lead

Angels – coins worth ten shillings

Apperil – peril, risk

Arcana – mysteries, arcane secrets

Argentata – cosmetic white lead

At all pieces – to perfection

Bermudas – disreputable area at the foot of St Martin's Lane

Blanks – French coins of low value

Borachio – Spanish bag for wine

Brach – female hunting dog

Bristol-stone – native British gem

Broad-clothes – plain woollen cloth

Broker's block – clothes-mount used by pawnbrokers

Cabinets – private inner rooms

Carats – value of a precious stone

Caroche – fine coach

Castle-soap – fine Castilian soap

Cautelous – wily

Chartel – written challenge

Cioppinos – shoes with high soles, fashionable in Spain

Cock stones – stones in the gizzard of a cock: aphrodisiac

Cog – card sharper

Cokes – simpleton (after BJ's own character in *Bartholomew Fair*)

Cornish counterfeit – supposed British diamond

Counters – debtors' prisons

Crack – lively young man

Crambe – crambo, word-game

Creaks his engine – 'sounds like one of his schemes'

Crisped – close-curled

Cut-works – kind of embroidery

Daw – torment

Denier – French coin of low value

Distaste – disagreement, quarrel

Doxy – criminal's mistress

E-la – highest note of the stave

Ensigns – flags for signalling

Equivoces – ambiguities

Escudero – Spanish guard

Feoffees – those to whom an estate has been made over

Feoffment – title deed to an estate

Figgum – juggler's fire-eating act?

Fizzling – farting noiselessly

French stick – ribboned walking stick

French-time – low bow, as in a French dance?

Fucus – cosmetic paint

Galley-pot – apothecary's vessel

Garnish – bribe

Gear – nonsensical trickery

Gimlets – carpenter's boring tools

Glebe – earth

Gleek – card game for three

Gliddered – glazed

Grant-parole – give leave

Guarda-duennas – lady's chaperones

Hand-gout – stiffness of hands, ie miserliness

Harrington – brass farthing, after their monopolist maker

Hum – a strong ale

Jew's trump – Jew's harp

Kell – cocoon

Kind – humanity, human nature

Lading – loading, ie burden

Laving – emptying

Leaden men – toy soldiers (of lead)

Leaguer – camp of besieging army

Livery and seisin – legal making over of property

Migniard – exquisite, delicate

Motion – mechanical show

Mulcted – fined

Nard – aromatic plant

Neal – anneal, strengthen by firing

Niaise – 'a young hawk taken crying out of the nest' (BJ)

Nupson – gull, innocent

Obarm – hot mead-based drink

Ore-tenus – by word of mouth

Pan – the central hollow (ie, where most water lies)

Parcel-Devil – 'partially a devil'

Perfect business – properly-conducted quarrel (ie duel)

Picardill – stiffened collar

Pinnace – small, trim sailing ship

Pomatums – fragrant ointments

Pounces – talons of a hawk

Pragmatic – busy, inquisitive

Puisne – small, puny

Purslane – herb used in salads

Purtenance – 'innards', guts

Put case – suppose

Rerum natura – 'natural things'

Ribibe – silly old woman

Rush – rushes (with which the stage was strewn)

'Say – essay, ie try on

Shop-shift – shopkeeper's trick

Skirts – borders, outer edges

Soused – swooped upon

Spruntly – trimly, smartly

St Pulchre's – church ministering to condemned criminals

Stoter – small Dutch coin

Stuffs – woollen cloths, goods

Succours – help, assistance

Sutler – provisioner to the army

Tall board – gaming table

Tentiginous – lustful

Toy – trick

Tract – attraction, pull

Trencher – wooden dish

Tunning – brewing (in a mash tun)

Un-to-be-melted – ie, unyielding

Undertaker – contractor

Veered – let loose, paid out

Venting – vending, selling

Vetus Iniquitas – Old Iniquity (the Devil)

Via pecunia – 'Out with money!'

Wafers – disks for sealing letters

Wanion, with a – with a vengeance

Wusse – indeed, certainly

Yellow starch – starch used for ruffs and collars